Effect of psychological stress on human macrophages

Ulrike Kübler

Effect of psychological stress on human macrophages

Bibliografische Information der Deutschen Nationalbibliothek

Die Deutsche Nationalbibliothek verzeichnet diese Publikation in der

Deutschen Nationalbibliografie; detaillierte bibliografische Daten sind im Internet

über http://dnb.d-nb.de abrufbar.

1. Aufl. - Göttingen : Cuvillier, 2012

 Zugl.: Zürich, Univ., Diss., 2011

 978-3-95404-108-4

This thesis was accepted as a doctoral dissertation by the Faculty of Arts of the University of
Zurich in the autumn semester 2011 on the recommendation of Prof. Dr. rer. nat. Ulrike Ehlert
and Prof. Dr. phil. Petra H. Wirtz.

Cover Image © Lev Dolgatsjov / Fotolia.com

CONTENTS

ACKNOWLEDGEMENT

First of all, I wish to express my deepest gratitude to my supervisor Prof. Dr. Ulrike Ehlert, who gave me the opportunity to conduct the studies for this thesis at her department. I thank her deeply for her valuable suggestions, her presence, which provided an optimal amount of opportunities for discussion and exchange, her goodwill and patience, and her constant faith in me during my entire dissertation period.

A special and enormous word of thanks is also due to Prof. Dr. Petra H. Wirtz, whose unfailing readiness to help, valuable and excellent scientific advice and support contributed decisively to the success of this thesis. I learned a great deal from her.

My appreciation also goes to Prof. Dr. Andreas Stemmer, head of the Nanotechnology Group at Swiss Federal Institute of Technology Zurich, and Dr. Miho Sakai who gave me the necessary expertise to perform laboratory analysis of the data presented in this work.

The fact that the days of examination in the laboratory were organized so successfully and beyond the scope of the daily routine is due to the great contributions of Susanne Huber, Angela Arpagaus and Rebecca Meister. Thank you for your tremendous commitment and many happy hours shared. I would also like to thank the following colleagues for their constant helpfulness, their encouraging words, and above all the enjoyable time: Dr. Elvira Abbruzzese, Suzana Drobnjak, Pearl Ghaemmaghami, Dr. Roberto La Marca, and Dr. Myriam Thoma.

Last but not least, I would like to thank my grandmother Berta Kübler, my parents Gabriele and Werner Kübler, my brother Steffen Kübler, and Stephanie Krendlinger for their unfailing support.

ABSTRACT

The present thesis aimed to investigate the effects of psychological stress on the microbicidal potential of human macrophages in order to shed more light on the mechanisms that underlie stress-induced delays in the progress of wound healing. For this purpose, two studies were conducted. In a first study, we implemented an *in vitro* assay to assess the microbicidal potential of human macrophages. In a second study, we set out to examine the influence of an acute psychological stressor on the microbicidal potential of human macrophages within a wound paradigm.

STUDY I

Quantitative and qualitative changes in circulating leukocytes are known to be linked to psychological states. However, there is little information regarding comparable results with leukocytes in peripheral tissues, such as associations between the microbicidal potential of macrophages and psychological states. In this study, we implemented an inexpensive, simple-to-use and valid *in vitro* method for measuring the microbicidal potential of *ex vivo* isolated human monocyte-derived macrophages (HMDM).

The method was implemented and validated using 21 healthy male subjects ($M = 35.0$ yrs; $SEM = 2.32$). The assay principle is based on the reduction of 2-(4-Iodophenyl)-3-(4-nitrophenyl)-5-(2,4-disulfophenyl)-2H-tetrazolium (WST-1) by superoxide anions (O_2^{-}), the first in a series of pathogen-killing reactive oxygen species produced by activated macrophages. First, freshly-isolated human monocytes were chemically stimulated to differentiate into macrophages. Subsequently, the HMDM were activated with phorbol 12-myristate 13-acetate to induce a microbicidal or O_2^- response.

The WST-1 macrophage assay induced O_2^- responses by HMDM in all of the subjects. Furthermore, the WST-1 reduction scores correlated closely with results obtained by a reference method. The findings suggest that the *in vitro* method implemented investigates the microbicidal potential of *ex vivo* isolated HMDM in a simple, cost-efficient and valid manner.

STUDY II

Acute psychological stress induces changes in circulating blood leukocytes, but its effect on leukocytes in peripheral tissues is largely unknown. Activated tissue macrophages are important in early phases of wound healing, in particular by killing microbes. We hypothesized that (a) acute psychological stress reduces the microbicidal potential of HMDM, and (b) these reductions are related to stress hormone release.

Forty-one healthy men (mean age 35 ± 1 yr) were randomized to either the stress ($n = 24$) or control group ($n = 17$). While the stress group underwent the Trier Social Stress Test (TSST; combination of mock job interview and mental arithmetic task), controls did not. Assessing the microbicidal potential, we investigated PMA-activated O_2^- production by *ex vivo* isolated HMDM immediately before and after stress, and during recovery up to 60 min after TSST / rest. Moreover, we repeatedly measured plasma norepinephrine and epinephrine levels as well as salivary cortisol.

The groups differed significantly in their HMDM microbicidal potential ($p = .01$) in reaction to stress. Post hoc testing revealed that while HMDM of the control group displayed a significant increase in O_2^- production over time ($p = .02$), the cells of the stress group did not ($p = .83$). Immediately and 10 minutes after stress, O_2^- production by HMDM was lower in stressed subjects as compared to controls (p's<.05). Statistical mediation testing revealed that higher norepinephrine levels mediated lower amounts of O_2^- responses.

Our results suggest that acute psychological stress reduces the microbicidal potential of HMDM probably by norepinephrine release. This might have implications for stress-induced impairment in wound healing.

TABLES

FIGURES

ABBREVIATIONS

A

ACTH   = Adrenocorticotropic hormone

ANCOVA   = Analysis of covariance

ANOVA   = Analysis of variance

ANS   = Autonomic nervous system

AP-1   = Activator protein 1

B

BMI   = Body mass index

BP   = Blood pressure

C

CA   = Catecholamines

cAMP   = Cyclic adenosine monophosphate

C_{Max} = Maximum current registered

CRH   = Corticotropin-releasing hormone

C_{Sum} = Sum of all current values

CVs   = Coefficients of variance

D

DAG   = Diacylglycerol

DC   = Dendritic cell

ΔCORT   = Cortisol stress change

ΔEPI   = Epinephrine stress change

ΔNE   = Norepinephrine stress change

DMSO   = Dimethyl sulfoxide

E

ECM	= Extracellular matrix
EDTA	= Ethylenediaminetetraacetic acid
EPI	= Epinephrine
ERK	= Extracellular signal-regulated kinases

F

FBS	= Fetal bovine serum

G

GC	= Glucocorticoids
GR	= Glucocorticoid receptors
GTP	= Guanosine-5'-triphosphate

H

HBSS	= Hank's balanced salt solution
HMDM	= Human monocyte-derived macrophages
H_2O_2	= Hydrogen peroxide
HPA axis	= Hypothalamus-pituitary-adrenal axis
HSC	= hematopoietic stem cell

I

ICAM	=Inter-cellular adhesion molecule
IFN	= Interferon
IGF	= Insulin-like growth factors
IKK	= IkappaB kinase
IL	= Interleukin
iNOS	= Inducible nitric oxide synthase
IP3	= Inositol triphosphate

J

JAK = Janus kinase

JNK = C-Jun N-terminal kinase

L

LFA-1 = Leukocyte function-associated antigen one

LPS = Lipopolysaccharides

M

M1 = Classically activated macrophages

M2 = Alternatively activated macrophages

Mac-1 = Macrophage 1 antigen

MAP = Mean arterial blood pressure

MAPK = Mitogen-activated protein kinase

MCP = Monocyte chemoattractant protein

MCS-F = Macrophage colony-stimulating factor

MDC = Macrophage-derived chemokine

MHC = Major histocompatibility complex

MIP = Macrophage inflammatory proteins

MMP = Matrix metalloproteinase

MPS = Mononuclear phagocyte system

MR = Mineralocorticoid receptors

N

NADPH oxidase = Nicotinamide adenine dinucleotide phosphate oxidase

NE = Norepinephrine

NF-κB = Nuclear factor kappa-light-chain-enhancer of activated B cells

NK cells = Natural killer cells

NO   = Nitrogen oxide

O

O_2^- = Superoxide anions

P

PAF   = Platelet activating factor

PAMP   = Pathogen-associated molecular patterns

PBMC   = Peripheral blood monocytes

PBS   = Phosphate buffered saline

PDGF   = Platelet-derived growth factor

PI3K   = Phosphoinositide Kinase-3

PKA   = Protein kinasa A

PKC   = Protein kinase C

PMA   = Phorbol 12-myristate 13-acetate

PNI   = Psychoneuroimmunology

PNS   = Parasympathetic nervous system

PRR   = Pattern-recognition receptors

PVN   = Paraventricular nucleus

R

RNS   = Reactive nitrogen species

ROS   = Reactive oxygen species

S

SNS   = Sympathetic nervous system

SPSS   = Statistical Package for the Social Sciences

STAT   = Signal transducers and activators of transcription protein

T

TGF	= Transforming growth factor
Th cells	= T helper cells
THP-1	= Monocytic leukemia cell line
TLR	= Toll-like receptor
TNF	= Tumor necrosis factor
TSST	= Trier Social Stress Test

V

VCAM-1	= Vascular cell adhesion protein 1
VLA-4	= Very Late Antigen-4

W

WST-1	= 2-(4-Iodophenyl)-3-(4-nitrophenyl)-5-(2,4-disulfophenyl)-2H-tetrazolium monosodium salt

1 Introduction

According to the view of modern behavioral and psychosomatic medicine, autonomous and hormonal changes which result from interaction between burdensome life events and individual factors (e.g. coping strategies) can lead to adverse health consequences with involvement of the immune system (Ehlert & von Känel, 2010). Research findings in the field of psychoneuroimmunology (PNI) partly constitute the empirical basis of this view. PNI is an interdisciplinary science that studies the interactions between the nervous, immune and endocrine systems, and particularly how these interactions contribute to health.

A large amount of research interest in the field of PNI is directed towards wound healing (Godbout & Glaser, 2006). It has repeatedly been shown that psychological stress delays skin wound healing (Walburn, Vedhara, Hankins, Rixon, & Weinman, 2009). An efficient immune reaction is essential, especially in early phases of wound healing. Only then can microbes which have penetrated into the wound area be killed and wound healing can progress normally (Rojas, Padgett, Sheridan, & Marucha, 2002). Although current findings suggest that the stress-induced delay of wound healing is associated with a suppressed immune reaction, the exact mechanisms underplaying this stress effect remain to be elucidated (Gouin & Kiecolt-Glaser, 2011).

A special type of immune cell, which is found in peripheral tissues and plays a major role in the wound healing process, is called the macrophage (Mahdavian Delavary, van der Veer, van Egmond, Niessen, & Beelen, 2011). Macrophages, recruited in early phases of wound healing, are characterized by high microbicidal activity, through which they kill potential microbes and prevent colonization of the wound (Mahdavian Delavary et al.,

2011). Moreover, they also promote inflammatory processes and hence generally increase the efficiency of the immune reaction locally (Martinez, Sica, Mantovani, & Locati, 2008).

Given that psychological stress can impair wound healing (Altemus, Rao, Dhabhar, Ding, & Granstein, 2001; Robles, 2007; Robles, Brooks, & Pressman, 2009; Walburn et al., 2009), and given the role of microbicidally active macrophages in early wound healing phases (Mahdavian Delavary et al., 2011), it might be speculated that psychological stress exerts at least part of its wound healing impairment by inhibiting the microbicidal potential of macrophages. However, the effect of psychological stress on the microbicidal potential of human macrophages has not yet been investigated. One reason for this lack of research may be related to both the absence of and familiarity with simple and cost-efficient methods for analyzing the macrophages' microbicidal potential.

Therefore, the aim of this thesis was to establish an appropriate method for the investigation of the microbicidal potential of human macrophages in a first step. In a second step, we set out to examine the influence of a psychological stressor on the microbicidal potential of human macrophages within a wound paradigm. It was hypothesized that this research project would shed more light on the mechanisms by which psychological stress delays skin wound healing.

The presentation is organized as follows: First the theoretical background briefly reviews the subject areas of macrophages, psychological stress and wound healing, which form the basis of this thesis (chapter 2). Following this, the data from the two studies conducted as part of the present thesis are presented (chapter 3). Finally, the thesis is concluded with a general discussion of the obtained results and their implications for future studies (chapter 4).

2 Theoretical background

In this thesis, three large subject areas are integrated, namely macrophages (section 2.1), psychological stress (section 2.2), and wound healing (section 2.3). Since each of these subject areas is quite detailed and complex in its own right, they are first presented in separate sections before being integrated in sections 2.4 and 2.5.

2.1 Macrophages

Macrophages are tissue-based leukocytes that can be found throughout the body in almost all lymphoid and non-lymphoid tissues (Gordon, 2007). They play a crucial role in both innate and adaptive immunity. Among other things, these cells are able to engulf and kill microbes, infected or unwanted cells, and to activate T-cells by presenting antigens. Moreover, macrophages are highly secretory cells. They can secrete molecules that promote or inhibit inflammation, growth regulation and hematopoiesis, influence lymphocyte function, affect tissue repair and turnover, act as autoregulatory factors or enhance the cell's microbicidal potential (Adams & Hamilton, 1984). The main effector functions of macrophages are illustrated in Figure 1.

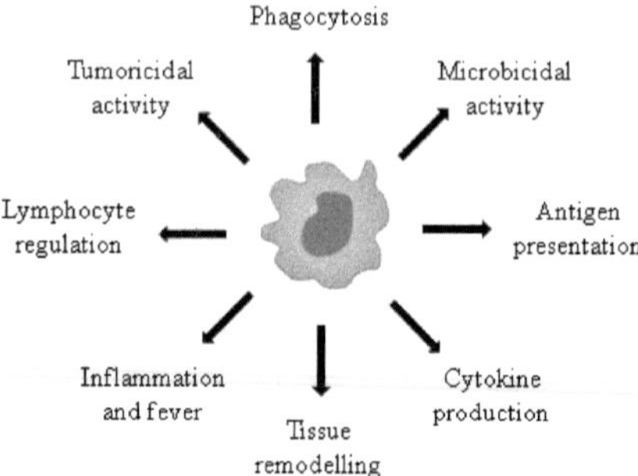

Figure 1. Major effector functions of macrophages. Adapted from Woods et al. (2000).

The following chapters will describe the characteristics and functions of these cells. Finally, practical aspects regarding the assessment of the microbicidal potential of human macrophages will be addressed.

2.1.1 The mononuclear phagocyte system

Macrophages are the terminally differentiated cells of the mononuclear phagocyte system (MPS). This system comprises bone marrow monoblasts and promonocytes, peripheral blood monocytes and tissue macrophages (van Furth et al., 1972). All cells of this lineage, together called mononuclear phagocytes, derive from a common pluripotent stem cell in the bone marrow, the so-called hematopoietic stem cell (HSC; see Figure 2).

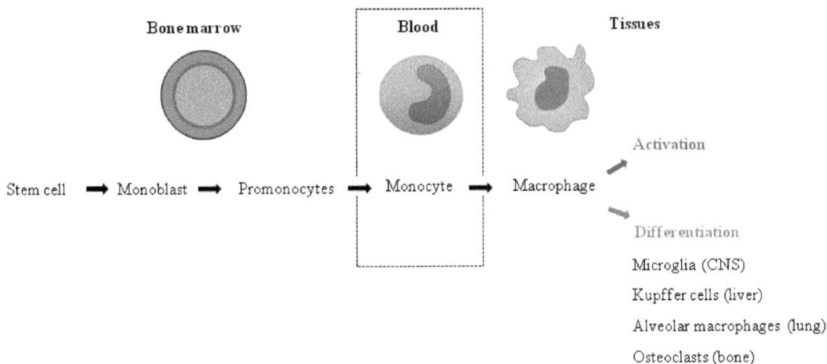

Figure 2. Differentiation of mononuclear phagocytes. Adapted from Abbas et al. (2007).

The primary function of the mononuclear phagocytes is phagocytosis. In addition, all cells of the MPS share further similarities in terms of functional, cytochemical, and morphological characteristics.

2.1.1.1 Monocytes and monocyte-derived macrophages

The precursor cells of tissue-based macrophages are monocytes. Monocytes, in turn, differentiate from precursor cells in the bone marrow (see Figure 2). This differentiation is orchestrated by sequential expression and action of different transcription factors, such as CCAAT/enhancer-binding protein β (C/EBPβ), acute myeloid leukemia, and IFN regulatory factor 8 (IRF8; Nagamura-Inoue, Tamura, & Ozato, 2001). The newly-formed monocytes remain in the bone marrow for about 24 hours before migrating into the blood (van Furth & Sluiter, 1986).

Monocytes circulate in the blood, bone marrow, and spleen (Auffray, Sieweke, & Geissmann, 2009). In humans, circulating blood monocytes represent 10% of the peripheral blood leukocytes (Auffray et al., 2009). Together with lymphocytes, they constitute the so-called peripheral blood monocytes (PBMC).

When monocytes migrate into tissues, they differentiate further into macrophages or dendritic cells (DC). This migration can occur either in response to an inflammatory stimulus or at a much lower level in the absence of any specific cues. Accumulating evidence demonstrates that there are at least two functionally distinct subpopulations of monocytes that can differentiate into tissue macrophages (Geissmann, Jung, & Littman, 2003; Gordon & Taylor, 2005).

In a murine model, it has been shown that under steady-state conditions, i.e. in the absence of inflammation, tissue-resident macrophages are generally differentiated from a monocyte subpopulation characterized as $Gr-1_{low}CX3CR1_{high}CCR2^-CD62L^-$ monocytes (Zhang & Mosser, 2009) (Tacke & Randolph, 2006). These cells are functionally most similar to human $CD14^+CD16^+CX3CR1_{high}CCR2^-CD62L^-$ monocytes (Tacke & Randolph, 2006), representing less than 10% of circulating blood monocytes (Serbina, Jia, Hohl, & Pamer, 2008). The migration of these monocytes into tissue under steady-state conditions contributes to the maintenance of constant numbers of macrophages in tissues. Notably, a further significant contribution to the maintenance of tissue-resident macrophage is made by proliferation of local progenitor cells (Daems & de Bakker, 1982; Landsman, Varol, & Jung, 2007; Mildner et al., 2007; Sawyer, Strausbauch, & Volkman, 1982; Tarling, Lin, & Hsu, 1987).

During inflammation, however, the dynamics of accumulating macrophages is considerably altered. Newly recruited blood monocytes, which differentiate rapidly into so-called inflammatory macrophages, contribute substantially to the increase of macrophages at inflamed tissue sites. Studying the origin and characteristics of skin macrophages during inflammation in a mouse model, van Furth and colleagues even found that 99% or more of the macrophages occurring in the inflammatory exudates derive from circulating blood monocytes (newly recruited inflammatory macrophages), while 1% or less originate through local proliferation of tissue-resident skin macrophages (van Furth, Nibbering, van Dissel, & Diesselhoff-den Dulk, 1985). The newly recruited monocytes typically correspond to $GR\text{-}1_{high}CX3CR1_{low}CCR2^{+}CD62L$ monocytes in mice or to $CD14_{high}CD16^{-}CXCR1_{low}CCR2^{+}CD62L$ monocytes in humans (Gordon, 2007; Tacke & Randolph, 2006). $CD14_{high}CD16^{-}CXCR1_{low}CCR2^{+}CD62L$ monocytes, also known as inflammatory monocytes, represent about 80-90% of circulating human blood monocytes (Serbina et al., 2008).

The recruitment of inflammatory monocytes from the bloodstream into inflamed tissue is a multi-step process, which is significantly mediated by adhesion molecules and cytokines.

Step 1: After the occurrence of different stimuli, such as interleukin (IL)-1 and tumor necrosis factor (TNF)-α from activated tissue-resident macrophages and bacterial peptides, endothelial cells express the adhesion molecule P-selectin on their surface within a few minutes, and then the adhesion molecule E-selectin with a time lag of about 1-2 hours (Abbas et al. 2007). On the other hand, monocytes express carbohydrate ligands for P- and E-selectins, which allow them to interact with the selectins on the endothelium. Selectin-selectin ligand interactions reveal a low affinity and fast off-rate. A stable binding of monocytes to the endothelium is therefore not possible. Instead, the monocytes "roll" along the endothelium as a consequence of this unstable bond (Abbas et al. 2007).

Step 2: A stable bond between monocytes and the endothelium takes place as a response to the interaction between the monocyte integrins very late antigen-4 (VLA-4; CD49dCD29), leukocyte function-associated antigen one (LFA-1; CD11aCD18), macrophage 1 antigen (Mac1; CD11bCD18) and corresponding adhesion molecules of the endothelium such as vascular cell adhesion protein (VCAM)-1, inter-cellular adhesion molecule (ICAM)-1-3, iC3b, fibronectin and Factor X (Imhof & Aurrand-Lions, 2004). This interaction is mainly promoted by the chemotactic cytokine monocyte chemoattractant protein (MCP)-1 (CCL2) bound on the luminal surface of endothelial cells. MCP-1 is secreted by tissue-resident macrophages and endothelial cells in response to microbial products, IL-1, and TNF-α. MCP-1 interacts with corresponding CCR2 (receptors for CCL2) on monocytes. This causes a conformational change of integrins on the rolling monocytes, thereby increasing the affinity of the monocyte integrins to adhesion molecule of the endothelium. A stable bond is formed between the endothelium and monocyte (Imhof & Aurrand-Lions, 2004).

Step 3: As a result of the stable bond, monocytes pass through the vessel wall and migrate into the connective tissue. This process is called diapedesis.

Step 4: The monocytes migrate along the chemokine concentration gradient to the site of infection and differentiate into inflammatory macrophages. Notably, the essential factor regulating the differentiation process from monocytes into macrophages is macrophage colony-stimulating factor (M-CSF; Hume, 2006; Hume et al., 2002). It has been shown that M-CSF is produced by both tissue cells and macrophages. Hence, macrophages can control their differentiation by using M-CSF in an autocrine manner (Popova, Kzhyshkowska, Nurgazieva, Goerdt, & Gratchev, 2011).

2.1.1.2 Macrophage activation during inflammation

In order to act in an effective way at sites of inflammation, macrophages need to be activated. Macrophage activation is the result of stimulus-induced modification of gene expression such that the functional competence of macrophages is either increased or acquired where it did not previously exist (Adams & Hamilton, 1984; Barish et al., 2005).

Traditionally, activated macrophages have been described as antigen-presenting phagocytes with high microbicidal activity and enhanced secretion of pro-inflammatory cytokines (Mosser, 2003). However, a series of *in vitro* studies investigating the macrophages attracted to inflamed tissue sites – that is, inflammatory monocyte-derived macrophages – revealed phenotypically polarized macrophages, depending on the stimuli used to activate them (Gordon, 2007; Gordon & Taylor, 2005).

Activated macrophages can differ in terms of receptor expression, cytokine production, chemokine repertoires and effector function (Mantovani et al., 2004). They are generally referred to as pro-inflammatory (M1) or classically activated macrophages and anti-inflammatory (M2) or alternatively activated macrophages (Mantovani et al., 2004; Pelegrin & Surprenant, 2009).

2.1.1.2.1 Classically activated macrophages

Classically activated M1 macrophages are characterized by an up-regulation of the surface molecules major histocompatibility complex (MHC) class II and B-7 (CD86; a costimulator for T-cell activation) accompanied by a simultaneous down-regulation of mannose receptors (this receptor binds mannose and fucose residues on microbial walls and mediates phagocytosis). Furthermore, their secretory profile is dramatically changed. They secrete high levels of pro-inflammatory cytokines, such as IL-1β, IL-6, IL-12, IL-15, IL-18, and TNF-α and therefore propagate the T helper cell (Th)1 response (Gordon, 2003; Martinez et al., 2008; Mosser, 2003). They also secrete high amounts of the chemokines CCL15/HCC-2 (for mixed leukocyte recruitment), CCL20/MIP-3α, CXCL9/Mig (for effector T-cell recruitment), CXCL10/IP10 (for effector T-cell recruitment), CXCL13/BCA-1 (for B-cell migration; Martinez, Gordon, Locati, & Mantovani, 2006).

Functionally, M1 macrophages display elevated endocytic functions and enhanced microbicidal activity, i.e. killing of microbes (Martinez et al., 2008). The latter is mainly mediated by increased secretion of microbe-killing, highly oxidizing agents, the so-called reactive oxygen species (ROS; e.g. superoxide anions [O_2^-]), and reactive nitrogen species (RNS; e.g. nitrogen oxide [NO]; Dale, Boxer, & Liles, 2008; Taylor et al., 2005).

Regarding their involvement in biological processes, it has been verified that M1 macrophages increase the magnitude of inflammatory processes and play a significant role during the early phases of wound healing primarily due to their pro-inflammatory and microbicidal activity (Mahdavian Delavary et al., 2011; for details see section 2.3). However, it is also known that uncontrolled activity of M1 macrophages is associated with chronic inflammation and tissue damage (Mosser, 2003). The latter is caused by synthesized radicals (e.g., ROS; see section 2.1.2.1) and by the proteolytic enzymes matrix metalloproteinase (MMP)-1, -2, -7, -9 and -12 secreted by M1 macrophages, which are known to degrade collagen, elastin, fibronectin, and other components of the extracellular matrix (ECM; Chizzolini, Rezzonico, De Luca, Burger, & Dayer, 2000; Gibbs, Warner, Weiss, Johnson, & Varani, 1999).

M1 macrophages are formed in response to interferon (IFN)-γ, alone or in combination with microbial products such as lipopolysaccharides (LPS), or further cytokines (e.g. TNF-α; Martinez et al., 2008).

Under physiological conditions, IFN-γ is primarily secreted by natural killer (NK) cells or activated Th1 and CD8+ cytotoxic lymphocytes (Martinez et al., 2008). The binding of IFN-γ to IFN- γ receptors on the surface of macrophage cells induces a change in the conformation of the receptor, which in turn activates the Janus kinase /Signal transducers and activators of transcription protein (Jak-STAT) signaling pathway. The Jak-STAT signaling pathway transmits signals rapidly and directly to the cell nucleus and to gene promoters that are regulated by IFN-γ (Schroder, Hertzog, Ravasi, & Hume, 2004). In addition to features characteristic of M1, such as the subunit genes of the enzyme complex nicotinamide adenine dinucleotide phosphate (NADPH) oxidase (i.e. gp91phox, p67phox, and p47phox), which is necessary for ROS production and thus microbicidal activity (see section 2.1.2), IFN-γ boosts transcription of the LPS receptor (toll-like receptor [TLR] 4) gene in macrophages, which primes the cells for a more rapid and increased LPS-induced response (Dalton et al., 1993; S. Huang et al., 1993; Sweet, Stacey, Kakuda, Markovich, & Hume, 1998).

LPS is the principal cell wall component of gram-negative bacteria. It is recognized by the soluble LPS-binding protein and delivered to a cell surface receptor complex that consists of the TLR 4 and the protein MD2 (Guha & Mackman, 2001). Several intracellular signaling pathways are activated in LPS-stimulated mononuclear phagocytes, such as

IkappaB kinase (IKK)- nuclear factor kappa-light-chain-enhancer of activated B cells (NF-κB) pathway as well as three mitogen-activated protein kinase (MAPK) pathways, which are extracellular signal-regulated kinases (ERK) 1 and 2, c-Jun N-terminal kinase (JNK), and p38 (Guha & Mackman, 2001). These signaling pathways directly or indirectly phosphorylate and activate various transcription factors, including NF-κB and activator protein 1 (AP-1; c-Fos/c-Jun), which in turn coordinate the gene transcription of many inflammatory mediators, such as TNF-α, and subunits of the NADPH oxidase (i.e. p47phox, p67phox, and Rac; Guha & Mackman, 2001). LPS increases the transcription of features typical for M1 via activation of these signaling pathways.

TNF-α is synthesized primarily by macrophages themselves as a response to LPS or IFN-γ (Takashiba et al., 1999). Like LPS, TNF-α contributes to the M1 phenotype via activation of the IKK-NF-κB pathway and the MAPK pathway (Huang, Krein, Muruve, & Winston, 2002; Takashiba et al., 1999). TNF-α is also known to potentiate the expression of the NADPH oxidase subunits p47phox, p67phox, and gp91phox und thus microbicidal activity of M1 macrophages (Gauss et al., 2007).

IL-10 and transforming growth factor (TGF)-β are some of the cytokines that inhibit the activity of M1 macrophages. These cytokines may be derived from adjacent cells or secreted from macrophages themselves following endocytosis of apoptotic cells (Fadok et al., 1998; Huynh, Fadok, & Henson, 2002).

2.1.1.2.2 Alternatively activated macrophages

M2 macrophages have been described in different variants, depending on the stimuli used to activate them (Gordon & Taylor, 2005; Mantovani et al., 2004; Martinez et al., 2008).

M2 macrophages are important for the late phases of wound healing and for dampening the inflammatory response (Martinez et al., 2008). As M2 macrophages are less relevant for the present thesis, these cells are only briefly described in the following (cf. Gordon & Martinez [2010] for a detailed description).

M2 macrophages are activated by the cytokines IL-4 or IL-13 often secreted by mast cells and basophils (Stein, Keshav, Harris, & Gordon, 1992). M2 type macrophages can also be activated via glucocorticoids (Mosser, 2003). IL-4, IL-13 or glucocorticoids induce a gene expression pattern that is almost the opposite to that of M1 macrophages via down-regulation of pro-inflammatory signaling pathways (e.g., NF-κB, AP-1, and STAT; Gordon & Martinez, 2010). Alternatively activated macrophages express larger numbers of mannose receptors and scavenger receptors, which mediate phagocytosis of microbes and endocytosis of oxidized and acetylated low-density lipoprotein particles (Mosser & Zhang, 2008). They also secrete the chemokines macrophage-derived chemokine (MDC; CCL22), pulmonary and activation-regulated chemokine (PARC; CCL18) and thymus and activation-regulated chemokine (TARC; CCL17) and suppress inflammatory processes via secretion of the cytokines IL-1ra/IL-1F3, IL-10, and TGF-β (Mantovani et al., 2004). M2 macrophages also promote wound closure by stimulating collagen synthesis (component of the skin; see section 2.3.1) in fibroblasts (Taylor et al., 2005). A key feature of M2 macrophages is their altered arginine metabolism (Mosser, 2003). While M1 macrophages synthesize the enzyme inducible nitric oxide synthase (iNOS), which catalyzes the metabolization of arginine to NO[1], M2 macrophages have increased arginase activity. The enzyme arginase converts arginine to ornithine - a precursor of the polyamines, which are involved in cell proliferation, and collagens (Hesse et al., 2001). Increased arginase activity and the associated consequences are one reason for the importance of M2 macrophages in the later phases of wound healing. Cell proliferation, which is also important in the later phases of wound healing (see section 2.3.2), is stimulated via secretion of platelet-derived growth factor (PDGF), insulin-like growth factors (IGF), and TGF-β from M2 macrophages (Gordon, 2003). Moreover, M2 macrophages are involved in angiogenesis, a process that is also important for wound healing, via these factors as well as the secretion of FGF basic, TGF-α and VEGF (Mahdavian Delavary et al., 2011). In addition, M2 macrophages are involved in Th2-mediated immune responses and thus associated with allergic reactions, asthma, and fibrosis (Duffield, 2003).

2.1.1.2.3 Functional plasticity of activated macrophages

Recent *in vitro* studies have demonstrated that a change in the cytokine environment is able to trigger a phenotypic switch from an M1 toward an M2 phenotype (Khallou-Laschet et al., 2010; Stout et al., 2005; Stout & Suttles, 2004). These findings indicate that macrophage activation is plastic, that is, it is reversible, and macrophages change their functional pattern in response to an altered cytokine environment (Khallou-Laschet et al., 2010; Stout et al., 2005). The functional plasticity of macrophages may have significant

---

[1] It should be noted that this statement is currently only established for mouse macrophages. However, it provides a lively forum for discussion in relation to humans. For details, see section 2.1.2.

implications for chronic inflammatory processes such as those often found in non-healing wounds (see section 2.3).

It must be pointed out here that mononuclear phagocytes *in vivo* are exposed to a wide range of stimuli, meaning that the polarization of macrophage phenotypes outlined in this thesis most likely corresponds to a simplification of the actual situation. It can be assumed that the M1 and M2 macrophages generated *in vitro* represent two extremes on a continuum of different macrophage phenotypes (Stout et al., 2005; Stout & Suttles, 2004). Nevertheless, this "simplification" provides a useful operationalization for the study of macrophages.

2.1.2 Microbicidal activity – effector function of M1 macrophages

As indicated above (see 2.1.1.2.1), a key effector function of classically activated M1 macrophages is their microbicidal activity (Hunter et al., 2009; Martinez et al., 2008). Macrophages can kill microbes either independent of oxygen, via the release of antimicrobial peptides / proteins and enzymes, such as defensins (Couto, Liu, Lehrer, & Ganz, 1994; Rogan et al., 2006), or dependent on oxygen, via the formation of reactive species (Halliwell, 2006). It is currently thought that the microbicidal effectiveness by macrophages is due in large part to oxygen dependent mechanisms (Dale et al., 2008; Nathan & Shiloh, 2000). For this reason the following explanation concentrates exclusively on the oxygen-dependent generation of reactive species.

2.1.2.1 Reactive oxygen / nitrogen species

The reactive compounds that generate macrophages to kill microbes, include both ROS and RNS. ROS is a collective term that comprises both radical oxygen compounds, such as O_2^-, hydroxyl (OH^-), hydroperoxyl (HO_2^-) and carbonate (CO_3^-) and non-radical oxygen compounds such as hydrogen peroxide (H_2O_2), hypobromous acid (HOBr), hypochlorous acid (HOCl), ozone (O_3), singlet oxygen ($1O_2$), and peroxynetrite ($ONOO^-$; Halliwell, 2006). RNS is also to be understood as a collective term. Radical (e.g. nitric oxide [NO^-] and nitrogen dioxide [NO_2^-]) as well as non-radical nitrogen compounds (e.g nitrous acid [HNO_2] and dinitrogen trioxide [N_2O_3]) are subsumed under RNS.

It should be noted that some compounds may be assigned to both ROS and RNS. These include $ONOO^-$ and peroxynitrous acid (ONOOH).

2.1.2.2 NADPH oxidase

ROS production is mediated by the membrane-bound enzyme NADPH oxidase. Once activated, NADPH oxidase transfers electrons from NADPH in the cytosol to extracellular or intraphagolysosomal oxygen molecules, resulting in O_2^-- a type of ROS (see above). This process is described in the following reaction diagram (El-Benna, Dang, Gougerot-Pocidalo, & Elbim, 2005).

$$NADPH + 2O_2 \rightarrow NADP^+ + H^+ + 2O_2^-$$

The O_2^- formed in this reaction is the starting product for further ROS such as H_2O_2, HOCl, and OH^-(El-Benna et al., 2005; Fang, 2004):

$$2O_2^- + 2H^+ \rightarrow O_2 + H_2O_2$$

$$Cl^- + H_2O_2 \rightarrow HOCl + OH^-$$

2.1.2.2.1 Structure of the NADPH oxidase

The NADPH oxidase is an enzyme complex made up of several subunits and is localized in both plasma and phagosome membranes in the activated form, that is, once its assembly is complete (see Figure 3).

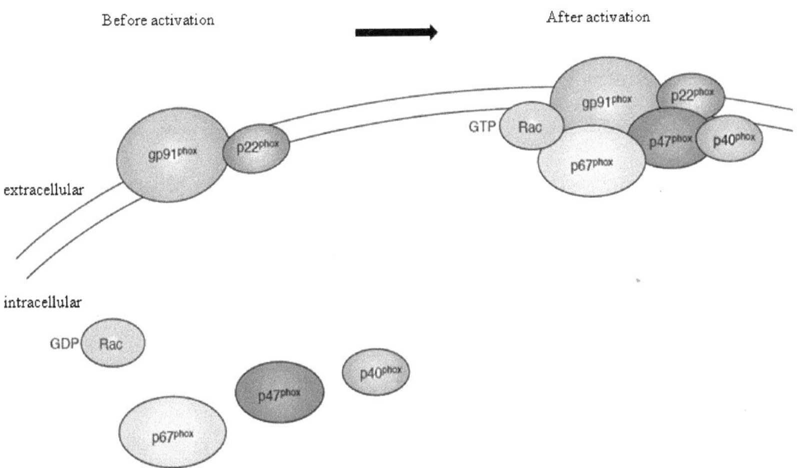

Figure 3. Schematic diagram of NADPH oxidase before and after activation. After phosphorylation the cytosolic subunits p67phox, p47phox, p40phox and p21rac translocate to the membrane-associated flavocytochrome b_{558} complex, which is made up of the subunits p22phox and gp91phox, and thus leads finally to activation of the NADPH oxidase. Adapted from Sakai et al. (2009).

The building block of NADPH oxidase is flavocytochrome b_{558}. This is a heterodimer comprising the membrane-bound subunits p22phox and gp91phox (Bedard & Krause, 2007). The prosthetic groups FAD and heme, which are involved in the transfer of electrons from NADPH to molecular oxygen, are bound by these two subunits. Other components of NADPH oxidase are localized in the cytosol in their non-activated state. This includes the proteins p47phox and p67phox (Cathcart, 2004). To be able to bind the membrane-bound flavocytochrome b_{558}, p47phox and p67phox must be phosphorylated by activated protein kinases, including protein kinase C (PKC; Bedard & Krause, 2007; Morel, Doussiere, & Vignais, 1991).

An additional protein that may contribute to NADPH oxidase assembly and activation is p40phox. It forms a complex with p67phox and also translocates to the membrane (Bedard & Krause, 2007). However, in cell-free systems p40phox is not necessary to induce the activation of NADPH oxidase (Babior, Lambeth, & Nauseef, 2002). For this reason, the precise role of this protein is unclear. It has also been demonstrated that following stimulation of the phagocytes the cytoplasmic protein Rac1 together with p47phox and p67phox are translocated to the membrane and then bind to p67phox (Bokoch & Diebold, 2002). Rac1 seems to stabilize the NADPH oxidase complex in an active conformation (Bokoch & Diebold, 2002).

2.1.2.2.2 Activation of the NADPH oxidase

The activation of NADPH oxidase, that is, the phosphorylation of the cytosolic subunits, is usually triggered by the binding of certain agonists to specific membrane receptors on the monocytes / macrophages.

The prerequisite for the process of activation, however, is sufficient quantities of cytosolic and membrane-bound subunits of the NADPH oxidase in monocytes / macrophages (Sakai et al., 2009). The transcription of the genes that encode oxidase subunits is controlled using various intrinsic and / or extrinsic molecules such as microbial products (e.g. LPS) and cytokines, including IFN-γ and TNF-α (Bedard & Kraus, 2007; Gauss et al., 2007; Schroder et al., 2004). Moreover, the transcription of the genes is associated with the degree of differentiation of the cells (Sakai et al., 2009). The group led by Sakai and colleagues (2009) has shown that the concentration of the subunits p67phox, p47phox, and p22phox in monocyte-derived M1 macrophages is more than three times higher than that in monocytes.

There are various agonists that are possible candidates for the actual activation of NADPH oxidase in physiological conditions. Examples of physiological agonists include complement factor C5a, platelet activating factor (PAF), LPS and leukotriene B_4 (El-Benna et al., 2005). These agonists are known to activate protein kinases, including PKC, which in turn promote phosphorylation of the cytosolic subunits and thus activation of the NADPH oxidase (Cathcart, 2004).

To be more precise, the receptor to which most of the physiological agonists are bound is in turn coupled to a guanosine-5'-triphosphate (GTP)-binding protein which then activates phospholipase C, D, and A leading to intracellular messengers (Bokoch, 1995). Phospholipase C, for instance, cleaves the phospholipid phosphatidylinositol 4,5-bisphosphate (PIP_2) producing diacylglycerol (DAG) and inositol triphosphate (IP3). IP3 binds to the membrane receptors of intracellular calcium stores which causes a rapid increase in the concentration of calcium ions in the cytosol. DAG activates PKC. The activated PKC can then catalyze the calcium-dependent phosphorylation reaction of the cytosolic subunits and thus the assembly or activation of the NADPH oxidase (El-Benna et al., 2005).

2.1.2.3 Nitric oxide synthase

RNS production is mediated by the enzyme nitric oxide synthase (NOS). NOS oxidizes L-arginine to L-citrulline and nitric oxide (NO·). This process is described in detail in the following reaction diagram:

L-arginine + 3/2 NADPH + H$^+$ + 2O$_2$ → L-citrulline + NO· + 3/2 NADP$^+$ (Kwon et al., 1990).

NOS is present in the cell as constitutive (cNOS) and inducible (iNOS) isoforms. The latter is found in macrophages and neutrophiles (Halliwell, 2006).

The activity of iNOS is regulated primarily at the level of transcription (Fang, 2004). For iNOS gene transcription the combined stimulation of so-called pattern-recognition receptors (PRR; e.g. TLR)[2] and pro-inflammatory cytokine receptors are required. These in turn activate several transcription factors that control the transcription of the iNOS gene (Stuehr & Marletta, 1985; Taylor & Geller, 2000). The NO· catalyzed by iNOS can directly kill microbes or synthesize other antimicrobial agents (RNS or ROS) in combination with O$_2^-$, as shown in the following:

O$_2^-$ + NO· → ONOO$^-$

---

[2] PRR located on the plasma membrane of phagocytes recognize conserved surface features of microorganisms, known as pathogen-associated molecular patterns (PAMPs; e.g. LPS). After a microbe binds to corresponding PRRs on the plasma membrane of macrophages, intracellular signaling cascades are initiated (Abbas et al., 2007).

Proceeding from ONOO⁻, further reactions are possible. Thus, ONOO⁻, under physiological pH conditions (7.4 pH) can be rapidly protonated to ONOOH. The resulting ONOOH from this reaction can turn into the two radicals OH˙ and NO_2 - (Alvarez & Radi, 2003). Alternatively, ONOO⁻ can also react with CO_2 (Alvarez & Radi, 2003):

$$ONOO^- + CO_2 \rightarrow ONOOCO_2^-$$

The $ONOOCO_2^-$ created in this reaction can eventually turn into the two radicals $NO_2^˙$ and $CO_3^˙$ (Halliwell, 2006).

As is evident from these different reactions, iNOS and NADPH oxidase represent two separate, albeit partially overlapping defense systems in macrophages.

2.1.2.4 Killing mechanisms

In microbes, ROS / RNS have different potential target molecules. In this regard, it should be taken into account that each of the ROS / RNS is characterized by specific reactivity, stability, compartmentalization and biological activity (Fang, 2004). Among the target molecules of ROS / RNS are thiols, metal centres, protein tyrosines, nucleotide bases and lipids (Nathan & Shiloh, 2000). The focus of the antimicrobial action of ROS is direct DNA damage. In contrast, the effect of RNS is primarily due to the inhibition of the respiratory chain and the disruption of DNA replication via inactivation of zinc metalloprotein. Furthermore, the ROS toxicity in microbes intensifies through the process of mobilization of iron from iron-sulfur proteins, which is in turn initiated by ROS and RNS (Fang, 2004).

However, it should be noted, that the precise mechanism of action of the reactive species *in vivo* has not been completely elucidated (Slauch, 2011). Also should be mentioned at this point that microbes have partially developed strategies that help them to avoid the damaging effects of ROS / RNS. These strategies include evasion, suppression and enzymatic detoxification of ROS / RNS (Fang, 2004).

2.1.2.5 Clinical importance

Despite the protection mechanisms of microbes and the lack of knowledge regarding the exact mechanisms of ROS / RNS, it is now considered that these reactive compounds play an important role in microbial defense.

The clinical importance of ROS in host defense is highlighted by chronic granulomatous disease. This is a disease in which the destruction of microorganisms by phagocytes (i.e. monocytes / macrophages and neutrophils) is impaired due to one or more defects in the genes that code for the NADPH oxidase – the enzyme complex that is responsible for the generation of ROS (Abbas et al., 2007). Clinically, these gene defects manifest as recurrent bacterial infections with microorganisms, including Staphylococcus aureus, Aspergillus fumigatus, Salmonella, Serratia marcescens and Burkholderia cepacia, perianal abscesses and fistulae, abdominal wall thickening with obstructions, granulomatous inflammations of the liver and inflammations of the bowel (Fang, 2004). The latter are difficult to distinguish from Crohn's disease. The cardinal symptoms for the gastrointestinal tract comprise vomiting, diarrhea, abdominal pain, weight loss, and fever. One option for therapy is the administration of antibiotics to control the infections caused by bacteria and fungi. The administration of macrophage-stimulating cytokine IFN-γ can also reduce the number of infections ("A controlled trial of interferon gamma to prevent infection in chronic granulomatous disease. The International Chronic Granulomatous Disease Cooperative Study Group," 1991). However, the mechanism of action is not fully established (Fang, 2004).

The importance of RNS in phagocytic defense can be derived from studies in knockout mice that do not express iNOS. These mice showed themselves to be more vulnerable to certain infections, including Mycobacterium tuberculosis, Listeria monocytogenes, Leishmania (several species) and Salmonella enterica (MacMicking et al., 1995; Nathan & Shiloh, 2000). In the human field, the importance of RNS for phagocytes emerges from polymorphism studies. It has been repeatedly illustrated that different iNOS promoter polymorphisms are associated with increased iNOS expression and resistance to malaria (Kun, 2003). Consistent with these findings, Lopansri and colleagues found that subjects with cerebral malaria had decreased plasma arginine concentrations (the substrate of iNOS) and a reduced NO synthesis (Lopansri et al., 2003).

Despite the obvious importance of RNS as antimicrobial agents, their role in human macrophages has sparked a controversial debate among experts (Murray & Wynn, 2011). While some authors consider the NO production via iNOS in activated human macrophages as virtually assured (for a review, see Fang, 2004), others are firmly convinced that human macrophages have no iNOS activity and therefore do not exhibit any iNOS-mediated NO production (Schneemann & Schoeden, 2007; Schneemann & Schoedon, 2002). The latter-mentioned authors accuse the former of not having specified the cell type responsible for NO synthesis. They also imply that the incorrect conclusions are the fault of the proponents of iNOS activity. Thus, the detection of iNOS mRNA or iNOS protein in human macrophages cannot be equated with the activity of the enzyme iNOS (Schneemann & Schoedon, 2002).

It should be noted at this point that according to current understanding, the activity of iNOS and thus the synthesis of NO· as the starting point for further RNS in human macrophages is to be regarded as doubtful, even though the iNOS activity in murine macrophages has been proven (Murray & Wynn, 2011).

2.1.2.6 Excursus: Reactive oxygen species as ligands for cell signaling

For a long time, it was assumed that ROS primarily act as a first line of defense against microbes. However, in recent years, extensive evidence has been gathered demonstrating that ROS also act as mediators of intracellular signaling cascades and regulators of gene expressions (Finkel, 2003; Forman & Torres, 2002; Hsing et al., 2011).

Several studies have demonstrated that in monocytes / macrophages, the activity of the transcription factors NF-κB and AP-1 is regulated by ROS (Gwinn & Vallyathan, 2006; Rojanasakul et al., 1999; Segal et al., 2010). Both transcription factors control the expression of genes, the products of which are involved in processes of inflammation. For instance, the transcription factor NF-κB controls or increases primarily the expression of pro-inflammatory cytokines, including IL-6, IL-1β, TNF-α and IL-8 (Hiscott et al., 1993; Li & Stark, 2002). Both NF-κB and AP-1 can be activated by H_2O_2, a representative of ROS. This indicates that there is a significant relationship between the amount of ROS produced and the extent of the inflammatory reactions (Iles & Forman, 2002; Kaul & Forman, 1996). In line with this, it has recently been demonstrated that the anti-inflammatory effects of propofol are based on the inactivation of NF-κB pathways, which in turn could be partially attributed to the down-regulation of ROS (Hsing et al., 2011).

However, it should be mentioned here that the specific response to ROS depends on various factors, including cell type and redox status (Dalton, Shertzer, & Puga, 1999). Furthermore, the molecular biological mechanisms underlying the ROS effect are not yet fully understood (Gwinn & Vallyathan, 2006).

2.1.3 Determination of the microbicidal potential – practical aspects

If the microbicidal activity, as an essential effector function of human M1 macrophages, forms the research subject, an assay should be used that allows conclusions to be drawn about the amount of certain microbes killed by human macrophages within a specified time period. An overview of such methods can be found in Bosco et al. (2000). If, however, as in this work, the microbicidal potential of human macrophages is the main research interest, the requirement for the microbicidal activity, then the amount of antimicrobial agents generated must be examined. In contrast to the very global measure of microbicidal activity, the microbicidal potential represents a much more specific measure.

For determination of the microbicidal potential of human macrophages, several practical aspects must be taken into account. In the following sections these aspects will be outlined.

2.1.3.1 Cell isolation, purification and differentiation

In order to investigate macrophages, the isolation of their precursor cells, i.e. the circulating blood monocytes, and their differentiation into monocyte-derived macrophages *in vitro*, is recommended in human studies. Although the isolation and investigation of tissue-resident macrophages is common practice in animal studies, for ethical reasons this is less common in human studies.

In practice, a two step process is often involved in the isolation of monocytes (Gessani et al., 2000; Handel-Fernandez & Lopez, 2000). Through density gradient centrifugation, PBMC (i.e., lymphocytes und monocytes) are first isolated from anticoagulant whole blood. Ficoll-Paque is appropriate as a medium of separation, because of its low cellular toxicity (edotoxins < 0.12 EU/ml; >90% viability of isolated cells), high yield (60±20% recovery of mononuclear cells from the original blood sample) and high degree of purity of the PBMC fraction (>90% cells present in the final preparation are mononuclear cells). Finally, in the second stage, the monocytes are purified, i.e. the monocytes are isolated from the PBMC. There are different methods available for this isolation, each of which has certain advantages and disadvantages. An overview of this plethora of methods of purification may be found in Gessani et al. (2000). One method for isolating monocytes from PBMC which is often employed, easily available and relatively cost efficient is made possible by the multitude of different adhesion molecules, e.g. LFA-1, Mac-1, that are expressed by monocytes. These adhesion molecules enables monocytes, after just one hour of incubation at 37°C, to adhere to plastic and glass surfaces, whether untreated or treated with different materials (Elsdale & Bard, 1972; Hassan, Campbell, & Douglas, 1986; Koller, King, Hurtubise, Sagone, & LoBuglio, 1973). The adherence of monocytes is promoted when, for example, during the incubation period, the PBMC fraction is suspended in a culture medium with a high serum concentration and low pH (Rabinovitch & DeStefano, 1973). After the monocytes have adhered to the surface, the remaining cells of the PBMC fraction can be removed, using a pipette to transfer fluids from the cell suspension, followed by rinsing. Rinsing is important, because besides the monocytes, other cells, such as lymphocytes, can adhere to plastic and other surfaces. However, their adhesion properties are not as strong as for the monocytes, so it is easier to wash them off (Gessani et al., 2000). Nevertheless, it must be assumed that using monocyte adherence to plastic or glass surfaces as a method of purification, no 100% pure monocyte population is to be obtained; that is, a small portion will be contaminated by lymphocytes (Gessani et al., 2000). Furthermore, it may be assumed that adherence constitutes a stimulus for monocytes that is known to influence the differentiation and activation status of the same, leading to altered functional cellular activity (Gordon, 1995; Paulnock, 1994). Table 1 gives an overview of these genes, which activity is influenced by the adherence of human blood monocytes to plastic surfaces.

Table 1.

Effects of human peripheral blood monocytes-adherence to untreated plastic on gene expression

Time after adherence	Genes	Effects	References
2h	IL-6	Increase	(Navarro, Debili, Bernaudin, Vainchenker, & Doly, 1989)
0.5-1h	IL-1β	Increase	(Sporn et al., 1990)
20-40min	TNF-α	Increase	(Eierman, Johnson, & Haskill, 1989; Haskill, Johnson, Eierman, Becker, & Warren, 1988)
30min	IL-8	Increase	(Sporn et al., 1990)
30min	IkB	Increase	(Haskill et al., 1991)
40min	Lysozyme	Decrease	(Eierman et al., 1989)
1.5-4.5h	M-CSF	Increase	(Eierman et al., 1989; Haskill et al., 1988)

Note. IL = interleukin; TNF = Tumor necrosis factor; M-CSF = Macrophage colony-stimulating factor.

Precisely because of this alteration of genetic activity induced by such adherence, this method of purification is not appropriate in some cases. With a view to macrophage differentiation, an additional 5 to 7 day incubation in a 37°C culture medium occurs, following purification of the monocyte population (Sharma, Sharma, & Bose, 2009). With simultaneous addition of IFN-γ, as well as LPS and/or TNF-α, to the culture medium, monocytes are differentiated to M1 macrophages (see section 2.1.1.2.1).

2.1.3.2 Induction of reactive oxygen species production

Given the fact that the microbicidal activity of human macrophages is primarily due to oxygen-dependent mechanisms and also iNOS activity and thus the production of NO in human macrophages is controversial, the detection of ROS is recommended for the determination of the microbicidal potential of human M1 macrophages.

As outlined in section 2.1.2.2, ROS production of M1 macrophages is dependent on the activity of the enzyme complex NADPH oxidase (El-Benna et al., 2005). *In vitro*, activation of NADPH oxidase can occur not only via the above mentioned receptor-transmitted mechanisms (see section 2.1.2.2.2), but also via non receptor-transmitted mechanisms. Thus phorbol 12-myristate 13-acetate (PMA), a non-physiological stimulus, activates PKC via the receptor-independent phosphoinositide kinase-3 (PI3K) signaling pathway, and thus, through the intermediate step of phosphorylation of the cytosolic subunits of the NADPH oxidase (Bedard & Krause, 2007). Due to non receptor-transmitted PKC activation, PMA makes possible analysis of microbicidal potential independently of individual differences with regard to the receptor density of the macrophages (Siddiqi, Garcia, Stein, Denny, & Spolarics, 2001). Furthermore, via PMA activation, a markedly higher ROS production in M1 macrophages is achieved than through activation by other PKC activators (Sakai, Vonderheit, Wei, Kuttel, & Stemmer, 2009; Siddiqi et al., 2001). One disadvantage is that with PMA, we are dealing with an artificial, non-physiological stimulus. Consequently, findings obtained using PMA have lower external validity than those derived from studies with physiological stimuli. Through LPS and diverse cytokines, such as IFN-γ and TNF-α, the level of NADPH oxidase activation can also be high, although notably lower than that obtained using PMA (Sakai et al., 2009; Thiele et al., 2004). Furthermore, synergetic effects of the combination of TNF-α and IFN-γ on the level of activation of NADPH oxidase in monocytes has been reported (Almeida et al., 2005).

2.1.3.3 Investigation of reactive oxygen species production

First, it must be clarified which ROS is to be determined as an indicator of microbicidal potential. O_2^- and H_2O_2 are among the first products of ROS produced by M1 macrophages (see 2.1.2.2). This is an argument in favor of determining them rather than other ROS that only develop after additional reactions. H_2O_2 is a relatively stable compound, and is therefore easy to determine. In contrast, O_2^- is unstable in aqueous solutions. Nevertheless, it does have two important advantages over H_2O_2. First, O_2^- is the product catalyzed directly by NADPH oxidase. Second, unlike H_2O_2, O_2^- cannot pass through the plasma membrane (Fridovich, 1997).

O_2^- can be assessed using various methods, such as chemiluminescence assays or spectroscopic methods. While with the first method, it is difficult to quantitate O_2^- directly, the second is extremely specific and sensitive. However, it does require an expensive apparatus and a complex experimental setup. On the other hand, the so-called colorimetric assays offer a sensitive and cost effective possibility for determining O_2^-.

Various reagents can be applied in O_2^- determination using colorimetric assays. One particularly appropriate reagent is 2-(4-Iodophenyl)-3-(4-nitrophenyl)-5-(2,4-disulfophenyl)-2H-tetrazolium monosodium salt (WST-1). WST-1 is a membrane-impermeable tretrazolium salt that can be reduced by O_2^- (Sakai et al., 2009; Tan & Berridge, 2000). The reduction of WST-1 results in the formation of a colored, water-soluble formazan salt with increase absorbance at 450 nm (Sakai et al., 2009; Tan &

Berridge, 2000). Consequently, the colorimetric measurement of formazan formation in the medium in which macrophages are suspended is a precise indicator of O_2^- induced WST-1 reduction and thus an indicator of M1 macrophage microbicidal potential.

An alternative to WST-1 is the reagent, cytochrome C. Like WST-1, cytochrome C is reduced by O_2^-. In its reduced form, it shows heightened absorption at 550 nm. However, compared to WST-1, it exhibits extremely high background leading to poor signal to noise ratio and low sensitivity (Peskin & Winterbourn, 2000; Tan & Berridge, 2000). Furthermore, unlike WST-1, cytochrome C interferes with H_2O_2 (Brandes & Janiszewski, 2005; Tan & Berridge, 2000).

In conclusion, to assess the microbicidal potential of human macrophages, an assay based on the reduction of WST-1 by O_2^- produced by PMA-activated human monocyte-derived M1 macrophages would be appropriate.

2.1.3.4 Available assays

As far as we know, there is currently no established assay in the field of PNI for studying the NADPH oxidase-mediated microbicidal potential in classically activated human M1 macrophages in a simple and cost-efficient way.

Recently, however, two methods for determining the quantity of O_2^- produced by PMA-activated THP-1-derived macrophages have been developed (Sakai et al., 2009). THP-1 cells are cells of a human monocytic leukemia cell line. These cells are similar to human monocytes in several respects, such as morphology, secretory products, oncogene expression, expression of membrane receptors, and expression of genes involved in lipid metabolism (Auwerx, 1991). The first method, a colorimetric assay, applies the salt WST-

1 to detect O_2^-. The other, in contrast, measures the quantity of current produced in a biofuel cell.

2.1.4 Summary

Macrophages are monocyte-derived tissue-based leukocytes. They play a crucial role in both innate and adaptive immunity. There are two kinds of macrophages, the so-called tissue-resident macrophages, which are continually present in the tissue, and the so-called inflammatory macrophages, which are only recruited into the tissue during processes of inflammation. The latter comprise more than 99% of all macrophages in inflammatory exudates. Depending on the microenvironment, macrophages can be activated classically (M1) or alternatively (M2). Presumably, M1 and M2 macrophages represent the two extremes on a continuum of different macrophage phenotypes. While the M2 macrophages resolve processes of inflammation, the M1 macrophages force inflammation to occur. Functionally, M1 macrophages display enhanced microbicidal activity. The microbicidal activity of human M1 macrophages is primarily determined by their production of ROS, which, for its part, depends on the activity of NADPH oxidase. NADPH oxidase catalyzes the oxidation of oxygen in O_2^- – the precursors of all further ROS. Through a colorimetric method, based on the reduction of WST-1, which is conditioned by O_2^-, the amount of O_2^- produced, and thus microbicidal potential of M1 macrophages – the necessary precondition for microbicidal activity – can be determined.

In the subsequent section the subject of stress is addressed, a definition is provided and the psychobiological stress response is outlined.

2.2 Psychological stress

Although stress is one of the most common psychological issues of our time, there is no standard definition for the term. Different views exist today regarding what stress means and how to define it, and none have been broadly accepted (Pacak & Palkovits, 2001).

For example, whereas the endocrinologist Hans Selye (1907-1982) defined stress as a "[…] nonspecific response of the body to any demand upon it" (Selye, 1974, p.27), Bruce McEwen, a neurobiologist, described it as an "[…] event or events that are interpreted as threatening to an individual and which elicit physiological and behavioral responses" (McEwen, 2000, p.173). In contrast, the American psychologist Richard Lazarus (1922-2002) characterized stress as a transactional process and defined it as a "[…] particular relationship between the person and the environment that is appraised by the person as taxing or exceeding his or her resources and endangering his or her well-being" (Lazarus, 1986, p.19).

In the following, a chronological overview of the most prominent definitions of stress will be given. Subsequently, the physiological changes induced by stressful events will be outlined.

2.2.1 Psychological definition of stress

Walter B. Cannon (1871-1945), considered as a pioneer of stress research, developed the concept of *homeostasis*, which he defined as the co-ordinated physiological process maintaining most of the steady states in the organism (Cannon, 1939). Based on this, Cannon conceived physical and psychological stress as factors disturbing homeostasis. Cannon also coined the term fight-or-flight response. In this regard, he postulated that physical and psychological emergencies evoke the activation of the sympathetic nervous system (SNS) and the release of epinephrine into the bloodstream with the aim of mobilizing energy to fight the emergency or to escape from it, and to subsequently maintain or reestablish homeostasis (Cannon, 1915).

Several years later, Selye extended the concept of homeostasis and introduced the *General Adaptation Syndrome (GAS)*, which describes three different stages of coping with a stressor. The GAS consists of an *alarm reaction*, which is analogous to Cannon's fight-or-flight response, a stage of *resistance*, associated with adaptation to the stressor and, when the exposure to a stressor is prolonged, a stage of *exhaustion*. Later, it was demonstrated that these changes are associated with and at least partly caused by the activation of the hypothalamus-pituitary-adrenal (HPA) axis and the subsequent release of glucocorticoids into the bloodstream from the adrenal cortex.

Selye's view that acute stress can protect the body, whereas chronic, prolonged stress can increase susceptibility to physical diseases and mental disorders is nowadays widely accepted. Both Cannon and Selye provided reaction-oriented stress concepts, and postulated non-specific, uniform stress responses. While Cannon popularized the SNS as a stress response system, Selye did so with the HPA axis. From a human science perspective, however, both authors overemphasized biological processes in their stress concepts and failed to recognize the role of mental processes. Therefore, the theories were of limited value for the explanation of inter-individual differences in human stress responses.

Presuming that stress results from a transaction between a person and its environment, Lazarus and co-workers developed a new stress concept: the transactional stress model

(Lazarus & Folkman, 1984). Two concepts, appraisal and coping, play a central role in this model. Furthermore, the model differentiates between primary and secondary appraisal (see Figure 4). During primary appraisal, a situation or event is judged as either positive, irrelevant or stressful for the individual's well-being. A situation is appraised as stressful when it includes aspects of harm, threat, or challenge. If the situation or event is perceived as stressful, the primary appraisal is followed by a secondary appraisal, comprising the evaluation of the perceived coping strategies / coping resources as well as the consequences of action. In addition, coping strategies can be subdivided into problem-focused or emotion-oriented strategies (Folkman, 1997). While the former are characterized by an active effort to solve a problem, the latter involve rather passive and avoidant coping strategies.

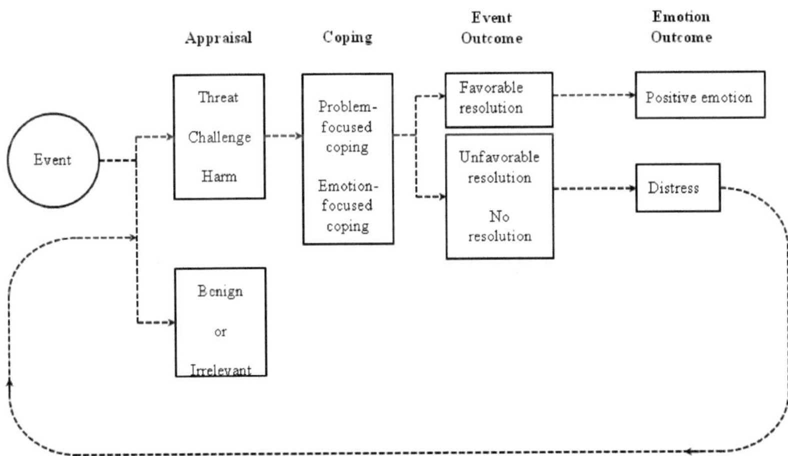

Figure 4. Lazarus and Folkman's appraisal model. Adapted from Folkman (1997).

Taken together, according to Lazarus, stress appears when perceived stressful demands of a situation (primary appraisal) exceed the perceived capability to meet these demands (secondary appraisal). Since appraisal is a highly subjective phenomenon and coping strategies are hugely individualized, the transactional stress model is able to explain why different individuals experience stress differently when confronted with the same situation.

The stress concept by McEwen (1998) provides an integrative biopsychosocial model describing the conditions under which physiological stress responses are health-promoting vs. health-damaging. The model comprises the constructs *allostasis* and *allostatic load*. Different to homeostasis, which reflects the maintenance of stability of a limited number of systems essential for life (e.g. pH, oxygen tension, and body temperature), allostasis refers to the process that actively maintains homeostasis. Most common allostatic responses involve the SNS and HPA axis. McEwen emphasized that stress-induced modifications in primary regulatory systems, such as the HPA axis and the SNS, are adaptive in terms of supporting the stability of those systems that are actually homeostatic. Allostatic load, in turn, describes the maladaptive consequences of prolonged activation of primary regulatory systems. McEwen described three conditions favoring allostatic load: (i) frequent activation of the allostatic systems, (ii) lack of adaptation to repeated stressors, and (iii) failure to shut off allostatic activity after stress.

For reasons of comprehensibility, in this thesis, stress is defined as a physiological response induced by stressors, which, in turn, are defined as perceived stressful events, real or anticipated, which disturb the individual's homeostasis.

2.2.2 Psychobiological stress response systems

The HPA axis and the autonomic nervous system (ANS), particularly the SNS, are the oldest and best examined physiological systems responding to stressors and are thus frequently identified as stress response systems. In the following section, both stress response systems and their biomarkers are outlined.

2.2.2.1 Hypothalamus-pituitary-adrenal axis

2.2.2.1.1 Anatomy, physiology, and cortisol

The HPA axis connects the central nervous system with the periphery via the endocrine system and comprises the following three components: the hypothalamus, or rather the paraventricular nucleus (PVN) of the hypothalamus, the anterior pituitary, and the adrenal cortex (Ehlert, 2010). In addition to experienced psychosocial stress, the HPA axis can be activated by numerous external and internal factors (Kirschbaum, 1999). When activated, corticotropin-releasing hormone (CRH) is secreted from the hypothalamus into the hypophyseal portal system. Then, CRH is transported to the anterior pituitary, where it stimulates the secretion of adrenocorticotropic hormone (ACTH) into circulation. ACTH in turn stimulates the adrenal cortex to release the glucocorticoid cortisol into blood (Ehlert, 2010).

The acute production and release of cortisol from the adrenal cortex into the blood can be essential for short-term survival. Cortisol primarily provides energy to cope with an immediate threat and to sustain basal homeostasis by stimulating the metabolism of glucose (Birbaumer & Schmidt, 2010).

In non-stressful situations, the HPA axis has a well-characterized pulsatile and circadian activity pattern deriving from connections between the suprachiasmatic nucleus (primary endogenous pacemaker) and the PVN (Buckley & Schatzberg, 2005; Kirschbaum & Hellhammer, 1994; Moore & Eichler, 1972). CRH is released with a frequency of about two to three pulses per hour and a peak of pulses in the early morning hours (Engler et al., 1989). Consequently, cortisol levels vary with the circadian rhythm, showing a significant rise within the first 30 minutes after awakening and a decline throughout the day (Edwards, Clow, Evans, & Hucklebridge, 2001; Horrocks et al., 1990). However, this circadian pattern is perturbed by changes in feeding schedules, activity, and lighting (Herbert et al., 2006; Tsigos & Chrousos, 2002). Therefore, the adult range of salivary cortisol level varies between 2-6 nmol/l (lowest levels at midnight) and 4-30 nmol/l (highest levels immediately after awakening; Tietz, 2006). The half-life of unbound cortisol in the circulation is about 80-100 minutes (Forest, 1989).

The level of circulating cortisol is regulated systematically in a long-loop negative feedback system (Miller & O'Callaghan, 2002). Through negative feedback, cortisol attenuates the secretion of ACTH from the pituitary and of CRH from the PVN. Furthermore, it exerts negative feedback on extrahypothalamic sites regulating both CRH synthesis and secretion (Owens & Nemeroff, 1991). In addition to the systemic regulation, cortisol levels are regulated locally by access to target cells and pre-receptor cortisol metabolism by 11β-hydroxysteroid dehydrogenase enzymes (Gathercole & Stewart, 2010).

2.2.2.1.2 Methodological impacts for cortisol assessment

The HPA axis can be stimulated by acute psychological stressors. However, stressors vary widely in their effectiveness to elicit an HPA axis stress response (Dickerson & Kemeny, 2004). In a meta-analysis of data from 208 laboratory stress studies, Dickerson and Kemeny (2004) examined conditions capable of evoking an HPA axis stress response. The authors found that motivated performance tasks characterized by uncontrollability and / or social-evaluative threat elicit reliable increases in ACTH and cortisol levels. Furthermore, the authors suggested that the Trier Social Stress Test[3] (TSST; Kirschbaum, Pirke, & Hellhammer, 1993), which comprises both elements, i.e. uncontrollability and social-evaluative threat, is possibly the best available stress test. The TSST induces a cortisol response in more than 70% of subjects (Dickerson & Kemeny, 2004).

Cortisol is considered as a reliable parameter of HPA axis activation (Hellhammer, Wust, & Kudielka, 2009). The hormone can be analyzed in different biological materials. However, approximately 90-95% of circulating cortisol is bound to proteins and erythrocytes (Kirschbaum, 1999). While only the free fraction of cortisol is biologically active, the bound fraction is inactive and serves as reservoir. In order to determine the total concentration (the fraction bound to proteins and the free fraction), plasma and serum are used (Cohen, Ward, Prins, Jones, & Venkatesh, 2006; Restituto et al., 2008). For the

---

[3] The TSST comprises a short introduction followed by a 5-min preparation period, a 5-min mock job interview, and a 5-min mental arithmetic task (serial subtraction) in front of an unknown panel of one man and one woman.

determination of biologically active cortisol (free fraction), saliva, urine or hair can be used (Zhang et al., 2008).

Similar to plasma cortisol, cortisol in saliva peaks about 20-30 minutes following acute stress exposure (Kirschbaum & Hellhammer, 1994). However, cortisol stress responses show large inter-individual differences and intra-individual variability. A recent meta-analysis investigated the role of different variables in salivary cortisol responses to acute stress (Kudielka, Hellhammer, & Wust, 2009). Among other things, age, gender, smoking, coffee, alcohol consumption, and dietary energy supply were found to influence the cortisol reaction to stress. In addition, altered regulation of the HPA axis activity and hence altered cortisol levels are associated with somatic and psychiatric conditions as well as with immunosuppressive medication (Ehlert, Gaab, & Heinrichs, 2001).

2.2.2.2 Sympathetic nervous system

2.2.2.2.1 Anatomy, physiology, and catecholamines

The sympathetic nerve constitutes one of the two efferent nerves of the ANS. The second is constituted by the parasympathetic nerve. Operating at a primarily unconscious level, the ANS regulates the function of internal tissues and organs in the body in response to changes in the internal and external environment. In contrast to the parasympathetic nervous system (PNS), which controls functions associated with rest and conserving of energy, the SNS controls functions associated with the fight-or-flight response. The control of the sympathetic and parasympathetic nervous system is primarily a reflex over the visceral afferent centers of the brain stem. In addition to this reflexive control, there are other, higher-level autonomic control centers. These include the hypothalamus, the limbic system and integration centers in the reticular formation (Trepel, 2004). Many organs are dually innervated by the SNS and PNS, such as the heart and the gastrointestinal tract (Birbaumer & Schmidt, 2010). Usually, however, one type of innervation predominates over the other. Similar to blood vessels, lymphoid organs receive predominantly sympathetic / noradrenergic innervations (Elenkov, Wilder, Chrousos, & Vizi, 2000).

The efferent, preganglionic nerves of the sympathetic nervous system originate in the thoracic and lumbar region of the spinal cord (Pinel, 2009). These preganglionic fibers terminate in sympathetic ganglia from which postganglionic sympathetic fibers run to the tissues innervated. Most postganglionic sympathetic fibers are noradrenergic fibers releasing norepinephrine (NE; Elenkov et al., 2000). The adrenal medulla contains chromaffin cells, and is anatomically homologous to the sympathetic ganglia. It is innervated by the neurotransmitter acetylcholine released from preganglionic sympathetic nerve terminals (Ulrich-Lai & Herman, 2009). Unlike the postganglionic sympathetic nerve terminals, the adrenal medulla mainly releases epinephrine (EPI), and, to lesser extent, NE (EPI/NE ratio is about 4/1; Birbaumer & Schmidt, 2010).

In response to a stressor, the SNS is almost immediately activated. Thereby, both the NE secretion from sympathetic nerve endings, and the EPI and NE release from the adrenal medulla into circulation are increased. By activating cardiovascular, metabolic, and neuroendocrine functions, NE and EPI mobilize energy to the muscles, heart, and brain, while simultaneously reducing blood flow to the skin, internal organs, and gastrointestinal system, and thus increase the organism's capacity for a fight-or-flight response (Birbaumer & Schmidt, 2010).

It has been reported that sympathetic activity increases during the day, from or before awakening (Narkiewicz et al., 2002). The circadian rhythm in plasma catecholamines (CA) follows the circadian rhythm of the SNS: decreasing during sleep and peaking in the middle of the day. CA circulation has a short half-life from ten seconds to 1.7 minutes (Molina, 2004).

2.2.2.2.2 Methodological impacts for catecholamine assessment

In addition to acute psychological stressors, such as performance tests, time pressure, fear, and anticipation of stressors, the SNS can be activated by a variety of other stimuli, including physical exercise, positive emotions, and exposure to heat, cold, electric shocks or noise. NE and EPI plasma levels have been established as valid biomarkers for SNS activity (Lundberg, 2000). The magnitude of the CA response seems to be closely associated with the intensity of perceived stress, regardless of emotional valence (Lundberg, 2000).

The response profile of CA due to psychological stressors such as the TSST is characterized by a rapid change of CA blood levels (within one minute after onset of the stressor), CA level increases to more than 10 times the resting level, and a peak at approximately 10 minutes after the onset of acute stress (Lundberg, 2000).

A small but virtually constant fraction of circulating blood levels of NE and EPI are excreted into the urine (Papadelis, Kourtidou-Papadeli, Vlachogiannis, Skepastianos, Bamidis, Maglaveras, & Pappasa, 2003). Consequently, NE and EPI can be determined not only in blood (usually plasma) but also in urine (Sluiter, van der Beek, & Frings-Dresen, 1998).

Inter-individual differences and intra-individual variability in the secretion of CA are associated with a variety of different factors. These include the intake of caffeine, alcohol, nicotine, and medication (e.g. beta-blockers), as well as heavy physical exercise (Lundberg, 2000). In addition, there are indications that plasma concentration of NE increases with age (Pfeifer et al., 1983).

2.2.3 Summary

In this thesis, the stress terminology reads as follows: a *stressor* is defined as a perceived stressful event that disturbs the individual's homeostasis, and *stress* is defined as an organism's physiological response to a stressor. The HPA axis and the SNS are the oldest and best examined psychobiological stress response systems. Both systems are known to be activated by stressors that are characterized as uncontrollable and that involve social evaluation. While salivary cortisol, the biologically active portion of cortisol in plasma, is considered to be a reliable parameter of HPA axis activation, plasma levels of NE and EPI are regarded as valid biomarkers for SNS activity. Inter-individual differences and intra-individual variability in stress-induced cortisol secretion and NE / EPI baseline levels are associated with a variety of factors, such as age, gender, smoking, coffee, alcohol consumption, and dietary energy.

Having discussed the subject of psychological stress, the subsequent section will give an overview of normal and impaired processes of wound healing.

2.3 Skin wound healing

A wound can be defined as the loss of the integrity of an organ as a result of exogenous or endogenous factors (Walburn et al., 2009). Wounds can be categorized on the basis of various aspects including i) etiology (e.g., mechanical, thermal, chemical causes or as a result of radiation), ii) duration (e.g., acute or chronic), iii) location (e.g., skin or mucosa) or iv) microbial colonization (e.g., aseptic, potentially contaminated or infected).

Skin wound healing is a complex and dynamic process with the aim of restoring tissue continuity in which various cell types, cytokines, growth factors, enzymes, and the ECM (e.g., collagen, elastin, fibronectin) interact in a finely tuned manner (Breitkreutz, Mirancea, & Nischt, 2009; Martin, 1997) and which is characteristically divided into four consecutive and overlapping phases: Hemostasis (formation of haemostatic blood clots), inflammation, proliferation, and remodeling.

The following provides a brief introduction to the anatomy of the skin as well as the characteristics of normal and disrupted wound healing processes.

2.3.1 Anatomy of the skin

The skin of humans is composed of two different layers: The epidermis, which forms the outer layer of the skin, and the dermis, which is below the epidermis. Keratinocytes are the predominant cell type in the epidermis. The dermis is a supportive, well-vascularized and nerve-rich connective tissue which anchors and supplies nutrients to the nonvascularized epidermis. The dermis is made up of collagen and elastin fibers. The former give the skin rigidity and the latter make it elastic. Both collagen and elastin are formed by fibroblasts which are also the predominant cell type in the dermis. As well as fibroblasts there are also immune cells in the dermis such as tissue-resident macrophages and mast cells (Mahdavian Delavary et al., 2011).

2.3.2 Normal wound healing

2.3.2.1 Phase I: Hemostasis

Immediately following an injury, a hemostatic blood clot begins to form in addition to hemostatic processes (Stroncek & Reichert, 2008). This clot is primarily intended to stop hemorrhaging caused by injury to the blood vessels and to protect the open wound surface from contamination from the environment. The hemostatic blood clot is made up primarily of thrombocytes and erythrocytes embedded in a network of fibrin fibers (Midwood, Williams, & Schwarzbauer, 2004). Thrombocytes are one of the first cells to mediate the activation and chemotaxis of macrophages via their cytokine secretions (Mahdavian Delavary et al., 2011). In addition to the chemokines RANTES (CCL5), MCP-1 (CCL2), macrophage inflammatory proteins (MIP)-1α (CCL3), which stimulate the infiltration of monocytes into the wound area, thrombocytes also secrete the growth factors TGF-β, PDGF, and VEGF as well as the enzyme thrombin (He, Blomback, Bark, Johnsson, & Wallen, 2010; Mahdavian Delavary et al., 2011). Thrombin indirectly stimulates adhesion and infiltration of neutrophils and monocytes by tightly regulating the expression of adhesion molecules (e.g., ICAM-1, VCAM-1) and pro-inflammatory cytokines (e.g., IL-6, IL-8) in endothelial cells (Kaplanski et al., 1997; Marin et al., 2001). Thrombin also stimulates the secretion of the pro-inflammatory cytokines IFN-γ, TNF-α, IL-1β, and IL-6 in peripheral blood monocytes via activation of the NF-κB pathway (Mahdavian Delavary et al., 2011; Marin et al., 2001; Rahman, Anwar, True, & Malik, 1999).

2.3.2.2 Phase II: Inflammation

The start of the inflammatory phase is characterized by hemostasis and the release of chemoattractants (e.g., chemokines, growth factors, products of fibrin proteolysis, and other matrix components), which attract phagocytes (that is, neutrophil granulocytes [neutrophils] and monocytes/macrophages) to the wound area (Mahdavian Delavary et al., 2011). Extravasation and migration of the phagocytes into the wound area is also boosted by vasodilatation and increased vascular wall permeability. These effects are caused by histamine which is secreted by mast cells in response to skin injury. In the inflammatory phase of wound healing the removal of potential microbes, foreign particles and cell debris is paramount (Mahdavian Delavary et al., 2011; Stroncek & Reichert, 2008). This task is initially carried out by neutrophils which are the first cell population recruited from the blood to the wound. One day after the trauma the neutrophils reach their peak concentration in the wound area, making up about 50% of all cells in the wound (Engelhardt et al., 1998). By secreting pro-inflammatory cytokines (e.g., IL-1α, IL-1β, IL-6, and TNF-α) neutrophils further promote a pro-inflammatory microenvironment at the wound site (Werner & Grose, 2003).

Inflammatory monocytes enter the wound area later relative to neutrophils and reach their peak concentration there in the form of macrophages about 48 hours after the injury, reaching 30% of the total cell number (Eming, Krieg, & Davidson, 2007; Engelhardt et al., 1998). Details of the process of extravasation of monocytes can be found in section 2.1.1.1. A few days after the injury the number of neutrophils declines drastically meaning that monocytes / macrophages are already the dominant type of leukocyte in the wound after 2 to 4 days (Engelhardt et al., 1998; Stroncek & Reichert, 2008). The primary task of the macrophages in the inflammatory phase of wound healing is similar to that of neutrophils; they stimulate an efficient immune response to remove potential microbes, foreign particles and cell debris and thus ensure a normal wound healing process. The cleaning of wounds is facilitated by the largely increased endocytic and microbicidal activity of the macrophages (Mahdavian Delavary et al., 2011). They also favor a Th1 immune response by increasing secretion of pro-inflammatory cytokines and attract additional leukocytes using chemokine secretion to ensure tasks in the wound area are completed efficiently. The efficiency of the immune response is also boosted by macrophages that present antigens which have been phagocytized by T cells and thus activate the adaptive immune response. Once cell debris, bacteria, and foreign bodies have been removed by macrophages from the wound, macrophages exhibit increased effector functions which are important for later phases of wound healing, that is, for proliferation and remodeling (Baum & Arpey, 2005).

2.3.2.3 Phase III: Proliferation

Re-epithelialization of wounds begins within a few hours after the injury. The proliferation phase is characterized by the formation of granulation tissue. The granulation tissue, composed mainly of keratinocytes, begins to migrate from the edge of the wound to the wound bed about three days after the trauma (Stroncek & Reichert, 2008). Here it forms a visible and delicate edge. These processes are also controlled by different cytokines. The growth factors PDGF and TGF-β, whose sources include macrophages (see section 2.1.1.1), stimulate fibroblasts at the edge of the wound to divide and migrate into the wound. The primary task of the fibroblasts that have migrated into the wound is to produce ECM such as fibronectin and collagen type I for the construction of the granulation tissue. There is also a sprouting of new blood vessels (angiogenesis) into the wound which ensures the tissue being formed is supplied with oxygen and nutrients (Stroncek & Reichert, 2008). Angiogenesis is induced by the growth factors Fibroblast growth factors (FGF) basic and VEGF which are secreted by the blood vessels themselves as well as macrophages and endothelial cells (Mahdavian Delavary et al., 2011). As soon as the wound surface is covered by a new layer of keratinocytes, migration of the keratinocytes ceases and they form a multi-layered epithelium. The growth factors epidermal growth factor (EGF), keratinocyte growth factor (KGF), heparin-binding epidermal growth factor (HE-EGF) and TGF-α are important in this process (Rodero & Khosrotehrani, 2010).

2.3.2.4 Phase IV: Remodeling

In this phase, which can last up to one year, scars are formed. This phase involves various remodeling and restructuring processes. Following wound closure some fibroblasts differentiate into myofibroblasts which are characterized by expression of α-smooth muscle actin (α-actin; Welch, Odland, & Clark, 1990). α-Actin enables myofibroblasts to contract which gives the wound tissue flexibility (Welch et al., 1990). With continuous collagen formation and degradation, type III collagen is replaced by type I collagen (Gailit & Clark, 1994). The collagen fibers are degraded mostly by MMPs which are produced by macrophages, fibroblasts, epidermal cells, and endothelial cells. In time, the number of fibroblasts and macrophages declines as a result of apoptosis. The large number of blood vessels also declines.

2.3.3 Impaired wound healing

Impaired wound healing in humans often manifests itself as delayed wound healing—in extreme cases as a chronic, non-healing wound (Eming et al., 2007; Rodero & Khosrotehrani, 2010). A prolonged inflammatory phase is associated with impaired wound healing (Eming et al., 2007). Moreover, almost all chronic wounds, despite having heterogeneous etiology, are based on defective progression from the inflammatory phase to the proliferation phase. In other words, the wound healing process often persists in the inflammatory phase in chronic wounds (Eming et al., 2007; Rodero & Khosrotehrani, 2010).

The prolongation of the inflammatory phase is characterized primarily by excessive infiltration of the wound area with inflammatory cells, that is, neutrophils and monocytes/macrophages (Eming et al., 2007). Bacterial infection, foreign bodies, and necrotic tissue have proven to be potent stimuli for excessive recruitment of these cells in the wound area (Eming, Smola, & Krieg, 2002; Singer & Clark, 1999). It can be assumed that the secretion pattern of inflammatory cells initiates a cascade of responses which create a microenvironment that impairs normal wound healing (Eming et al., 2007). A primary feature of non-healing wounds is an imbalance between proteases and protease inhibitors in the wound area (Saarialho-Kere, 1998). Elevated levels of proteolytic activity lead to degradation of the growth factors and structural proteins which make up the ECM and which are essential for the healing of the tissue. Macrophages and neutrophils are amongst the major producers of many proteases (e.g., MMP-1, MMP-2, MMP-7; see section 2.1.1.2). Given that pro-inflammatory cytokines stimulate the expression of MMP in inflammatory cells and inflammatory cells themselves are producers of pro-inflammatory cytokines, these mutually reinforcing processes can very quickly create a wound environment with high MMP activity. Chronic wounds are also characterized by an increased pro-oxidant microenvironment, that is, more ROS are generated than are captured. The major producers of ROS apart from macrophages are neutrophils. It can be assumed that an elevated concentration of ROS in the wound area interferes with the wound healing process both directly and indirectly (Wlaschek & Scharffetter-Kochanek, 2005). For one, ROS are highly reactive, meaning that they can directly damage cell membranes and ECM components. ROS can also stimulate the expression of pro-inflammatory cytokines (IL-1, IL-6, and TNF-α), chemokines, and proteolytic enzymes (including MMPs) via selective activation of specific signaling pathways and transcription factors (e.g., NF-κB) which in turn generates an inflammatory wound environment (see section 2.1.2.1.2).

2.3.4 Summary

Skin wound healing characteristically runs in four consecutive and overlapping phases: Hemostasis (formation of hemostatic blood clots), inflammation, proliferation, and remodeling.

Immediately following an injury the hemostasis phase begins with formation of a hemostatic blood clot This blood clot is made up primarily of thrombocytes releasing different inflammatory mediators (e.g. the enzyme thrombin), which in turn promote a pro-inflammatory microenvironment, as well as infiltration of neutrophils and monocytes into the wound area. Attraction of these cells to the wound area characterizes the start of the inflammatory phase that begins about 1 hour after wound administration. In this phase, the elimination of potential microbes, foreign particles and cell debris is paramount. This task is at first taken over by neutrophils, but 48 hours after the inflicting of the wound it is clearly taken over by macrophages. After the wound has been cleaned, the processes involved in the proliferation phase increasingly play a important role. Characteristic of the proliferation phase is the buildup of granular tissue, which finally closes the wound. The buildup of granular tissue is primarily supported by growth factors, produced amongst others by macrophages. In the last phase of wound healing, the remodeling phase, various remodeling and restructuring processes appear. The wound tissue becomes increasingly flexible.

Impaired wound healing in humans often manifests itself as delayed wound healing. In non-healing wounds the healing process frequently persists in the inflammatory phase. This prolongation of the inflammatory phase is associated with excessive infiltration of the wound area with neutrophils and monocytes / macrophages. Especially bacterial infections are potent stimuli for excessive recruitment of these inflammatory cells in the wound area. It is assumed that the secretory products of neutrophils and monocytes / macrophages initiates a cascade of responses which create a microenvironment that impairs normal wound healing.

The following section will integrate the three topics that were presented above on macrophages, psychological stress and wound healing.

2.4 Stress, macrophages and wound healing

Stress-induced modulations of immunological parameters, and the potential consequences for health, are transmitted over a complex network of different signals which, in turn, result from bidirectional communication among the immune, nervous and endocrine systems.

Since this thesis focuses primarily on the impact of acute psychological stress on the microbicidal potential of human macrophages, it is limited to the portrayal of this unidirectional relationship in the section below, meaning that the bidirectional communication between the nervous, immune and endocrine system is neglected. This is followed by two sections outlining the importance of macrophages in wound healing on the one hand and empirical studies on the influence of psychological stress on wound healing on the other.

2.4.1 Influence of psychological stress on monocytes / macrophages

Both monocytes and macrophages express receptors for many neuroendocrine stress hormones (Barish et al., 2005; Reyes-Garcia & Garcia-Tamayo, 2009; Rouppe van der Voort, Kavelaars, van de Pol, & Heijnen, 2000; Woods, 2000). This suggests that monocytes / macrophages are susceptible to psychological stress. The following discussion will focus primarily on NE / EPI and the glucocorticoids (GC) as stress hormones, as these hormones were investigated in this thesis.

2.4.1.1 Influence of catecholamines on monocytes / macrophages

EPI and NE mediate their action on monocytes / macrophages via adrenergic receptors. Adrenergic receptors are typical G-protein-coupled receptors. They are differentiated into alpha and beta adrenergic receptors. Both receptor types are expressed by monocytes as well as macrophages (Reyes-Garcia & Garcia-Tamayo, 2009; Rouppe van der Voort, Kavelaars, van de Pol, & Heijnen, 1999). While the stimulation of alpha adrenergic receptors mostly has an immunostimulatory effect on monocytes / macrophages, the stimulation of beta adrenergic receptors results in primarily immunosuppressive effects (Reyes-Garcia & Garcia-Tamayo, 2009). If both receptor types are stimulated at the same time, the beta adrenergic effects tend to dominate over those of the alphas (Reyes-Garcia & Garcia-Tamayo, 2009). Both groups each have several members which interact with different inhibitory and stimulatory G-proteins and thus also with different sequential intracellular signal responses (see Figure 5).

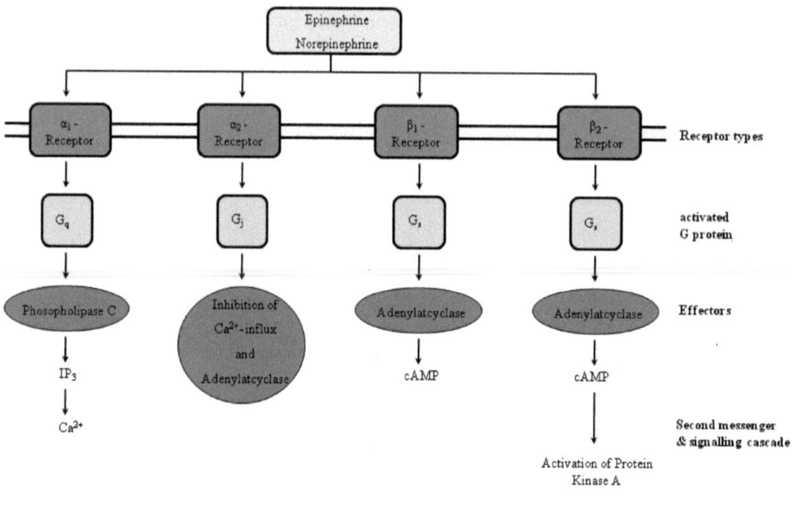

Figure 5. Intracellular signaling cascades induced by epinephrine and norepinephrine. G_q = G protein that activates phospholipase C; G_s = stimulatory G protein; G_i = inhibitory G protein; IP_3 = inositol triphosphate; cAMP = cyclic adenosine monophosphate; Ca^{2+} = calcium ion. Adapted from Schartl, Gessler, & Eckardstein (2009).

Alpha-1 adrenergic receptors couple to G-proteins of the subtype G-alpha q/11. Phospholipase C is stimulated via G-alpha q/11 following binding of EPI or NE to alpha-1 adrenergic receptors. This leads to an increase in the intracellular IP3 concentration and subsequently to an increase in intracellular calcium ions. Calcium ions play a crucial role in the intracellular transmission of signals. They are known to increase the activity of PKC, which in turn is involved, among other things, in the activation of NADPH oxidase (see section 2.1.2.2.2). The binding of CA to alpha-2 adrenergic receptors leads to a decrease in cyclic adenosine monophosphate (cAMP), which promotes the production of

TNF-α, IL-1, and IL-6 through the activation of PKC, and subsequent activation of NF-κB (Reyes-Garcia & Garcia-Tamayo, 2009).

On the other hand, the binding of NE / EPI to beta-1 and beta-2 adrenergic receptors is known to activate adenylate cyclase via stimulatory G-alpha proteins, which then mediates an increase in intracellular levels of cAMP. Like calcium ions, cAMP is an intracellular signaling molecule which is involved in the activation of protein kinases in particular. If the elevation of the cAMP level is mediated by the binding of NE / EPI to beta-2 adrenergic receptors, this results in activation of the protein kinase A (PKA) enzyme, which inhibits the transcription of NF-κB regulated pro-inflammatory genes (Reyes-Garcia & Garcia-Tamayo, 2009). In monocytes, the stimulation of beta-2 adrenergic receptors possibly mediates the expression of IL-10 via cAMP (Beck et al., 2004). If the cAMP level is increased by the binding of NE / EPI to beta-1 adrenergic receptors, however, this increase in the concentration results in the opening of calcium ion channels and subsequently to an influx of calcium ions into the cell (Reyes-Garcia & Garcia-Tamayo, 2009).

EPI and NE have often been reported as having an inhibitory effect on monocytes / macrophages (Reyes-Garcia & Garcia-Tamayo, 2009). NE promotes the TH2-type cytokine response, i.e. the release of cytokines IL-4 and IL-10 (Mamessier et al., 2007). Linked to this is a reduction in phagocytosis in macrophages as well as a reduced production of O_2^- (see also section 2.1.1.2; Reyes-Garcia & Garcia-Tamayo, 2009) – presumably through the promotion of the alternative macrophage activation. Moreover, it is possible to inhibit the production of cytokines IL-1, IL-6 and TNF-α through the electrically induced release of NE. This effect is presumably mediated by beta-2 receptors. Furthermore, NE has been repeatedly shown to inhibit LPS-induced production of pro-inflammatory cytokines such as TNF-α in monocytes as well as in macrophages (van der Poll, Jansen, Endert, Sauerwein, & van Deventer, 1994; Verhoeckx, Doornbos, van der Greef, Witkamp, & Rodenburg, 2005). In human monocytes, it was shown that EPI increases the expression of the anti-inflammatory cytokine IL-10 and reduces the expression of TNF-α due to an elevation in cAMP, induced by beta receptors (Muthu, Deng, Gamelli, Shankar, & Jones, 2005).

Notwithstanding this, there have also been occasional findings that show the activating effect of NE and EPI on monocytes / macrophages. Takahashi and colleagues reported, for instance, an elevated release of the cytokines IL-18, TNF-α and IFN-γ in monocytes, induced by a beta-2 adrenergic agonist (Takahashi et al., 2004). The group led by Ortega also reported an elevation in O_2^- production in peritoneal macrophages in mice after incubation with NE *in vitro* (Ortega, Garcia, Saez, & De la Fuente, 2000). However, this finding could not be confirmed by Garcia and colleagues. These authors were unable to report O_2^- production influenced by NE in either PMA-stimulated or un-stimulated mouse macrophages in their *in vitro* experiment (Garcia, del Carmen Saez, De la Fuente, & Ortega, 2003).

2.4.1.2 Influence of glucocorticoids on monocytes / macrophages

GC are considered to be stimuli that promote the differentiation of monocytes into alternatively activated M2 macrophages (see section 2.1.1.2.2; Ehrchen et al., 2007). Against this background, it is unsurprising that several groups of authors have reported anti-inflammatory GC effects on monocytes / macrophages (Auphan, DiDonato, Rosette, Helmberg, & Karin, 1995; Scheinman, Cogswell, Lofquist, & Baldwin, 1995; Steer, Kroeger, Abraham, & Joyce, 2000). Stanojevic and colleagues also found *in vitro* a dose-dependent reduction in ROS production in peritoneal macrophages in rats (Stanojevic, Mitic, Vujic, Kovacevic-Jovanovic, & Dimitrijevic, 2007). Similarly, Ehrchen and colleagues found a decrease in spontaneous as well as PMA-induced production of ROS in GC-treated human monocytes (Ehrchen et al., 2007). In a further study, human monocytes, which following 24-48 hours of incubation with dexamethasone, a synthetic member of the glucocorticoid class of steroid, were incubated for a further six hours with LPS, showed a reduced expression of the pro-inflammatory cytokines TNF-α and IFN-γ (Cepika et al., 2010). Interestingly, there is evidence that the expression of beta-2 adrenergic receptors on macrophages is elevated by cortisol (Straub, Westermann, Scholmerich, & Falk, 1998). As reported above, beta-2 adrenergic receptors in monocytes and macrophages primarily induce effects that inhibit inflammatory reactions. In light of these findings, one could speculate that a part of the anti-inflammatory GC effect is mediated by NE / EPI. However, the effect of GC on monocytes / macrophages can be modulated by various factors, including cytokines or GC concentrations.

Lower GC concentrations appear to boost ROS production in monocytes / macrophages (Stanojevic et al., 2007). The effect of GC may also be dependent on the activation status of the monocytes / macrophages. Stanojevic and colleagues demonstrated that prior exposure of rats to a stressor (i.e. acute exposure to electric tail shock stress or exposure to a stress-witnessing procedure) alters the responsiveness of the isolated tissue-resident macrophages to their *in vitro* treatment with corticosterone. The cells were less sensitive to corticosterone. In other words, while macrophages isolated from unstressed rats showed a GC-induced decrease in ROS production, this GC effect was diminished in macrophages isolated from rats exposed to a stressor 24 hours earlier (Stanojevic et al., 2007). This partly contradictory activity profile for GC can be better understood if one considers the mechanisms by which GC exert their effects on monocytes / macrophages.

The molecular mechanisms by which GC affect monocytes / macrophages can be divided into genomic mechanisms and non-genomic mechanisms. The former include effects of GC on the expression of target genes while the latter include effects of GC on degrees of activation and responsiveness of target cells (Perretti & D'Acquisto, 2009). While the genomic mode of action is associated with a delayed cell response starting between tens of minutes to hours after cell exposure to GC, the non-genomic mode of action is associated with a rapid (within seconds to minutes) response to GC (George, Schiltz, & Hager, 2009; Urbach, Verriere, Grumbach, Bousquet, & Harvey, 2006). The genomic action of GC on monocytes / macrophages is mediated through binding to two types of hormone-activated transcription factors, the low-affinity glucocorticoid receptor (GR) and the ten-fold higher affinity mineralocorticoid receptor (MR; Beato, Herrlich, & Schutz, 1995; Nagalski & Kiersztan, 2010).

Having a full genomic effect, GC diffuse in their target cells, where they bind inactive cytosolic glucocorticoid receptors (GR) or mineralocorticoid receptors (MR) in association with heat-shock proteins. After ligand binding, the GC-GR and / or GC-MR complex undergoes conformational change, resulting in dissociation of heat-shock proteins. This leads to activation of the GC-GR and / or GC-MR complex, rendering it able to translocate into the nucleus, where it can dimerize and bind to target elements, glucocorticoid response elements (GREs; specific nucleotide sequences), and / or other transcription factors in the promoter region of GC-responsive genes (DeRijk, Schaaf, & de Kloet, 2002). Through different complicated mechanisms, the bound GC-GR and / or GC-

MR complex can then directly or indirectly regulate the gene expression via modulating transcription (Barnes, 2010; DeRijk et al., 2002).

Despite their preference for the same ligands and DNA binding sites, MR and GR influence different, virtually complementary transcriptional programs, which results in a complex activity profile on the cells (Barish et al., 2005). This complexity is increased by the fact that the expression of GR and MR can differ depending on the activating stimulus. While LPS in macrophages, for example, induces an elevated expression of GR, the expression of MR drastically reduces after only two hours. The situation is further complicated by the fact that the effects of GC-MR on macrophages are unknown (Barish et al., 2005). The anti-inflammatory effects induced in macrophages by GC-GR are, however, considered to be well established. It is worth mentioning that due to alternative splicing of the GR transcript (mRNA), four GR isoforms (variants) may occur: GRα, GRβ, GRδ, and GRγ (Grzanka, Misiolek, Golusinski, & Jarzab, 2011). Among these isoforms, the GRα isoform represents the only active form. The GRβ, however, is discussed to inhibit signaling pathways of active GRα by several mechanisms which possibly lead to a secondary resistance to GC (Grzanka et al., 2011). Interestingly, previous studies have shown that pro-inflammatory cytokines, such as IL-1 and TNF-α, promote alternative splicing of the GR transcript and consequently enhance GRβ expression. The biological significance of GRδ and GRγ has yet to be studied (Grzanka et al., 2011).

Regarding the non-genomic action of GC, there is increasing evidence that these effects are mediated with and without receptor involvement (Grzanka et al., 2011). The latter mechanism may be based on nonspecific interactions between GC and cellular membranes, resulting in the activation of secondary messengers (Buttgereit & Scheffold, 2002). The other part of non-genomic GC effects is mediated by both membrane glucocorticoid receptors (mGR) and cytoplasmic glucocorticoid receptors (cGR). Activated mGR influence the activity state as well as the responsiveness of target cells by at least two processes: first, by interacting with ion channel proteins, and second, by stimulating synthesis of secondary messengers (Grzanka et al., 2011). Furthermore, rapid GC effects might also occur as a result of specific interaction with cGR. Regarding this mechanism, there is evidence that binding of GC to cGR can lead to intracellular signaling of components of other proteins (Croxtall, Choudhury, & Flower, 2000).

2.4.1.3 Influence of psychological stress on the microbicidal potential of monocytes / macrophages

Although susceptibility of human monocytes / macrophages to stress hormones has been empirically established, the influence of psychological stress on the microbicidal potential of human macrophages has not yet been the subject of research.

Moreover, only a small number of studies have been conducted in rodents, with inconsistent findings. While two groups of authors reported, after exposure to stress *in vivo*, a decreased ROS production by tissue-resident macrophages *in vitro* (Persoons et al., 1997; Stanojevic et al., 2007), another group found a stress-related increase in ROS (Palermo-Neto, de Oliveira Massoco, & Robespierre de Souza, 2003).

2.4.2 Significance of macrophages in wound healing

As is evident from the descriptions in section 2.3, macrophages are involved in various processes in normal and impaired skin wound healing. A wide range of important immunological functions are executed by these cells. In light of these findings, it seems obvious that macrophages make a critical contribution to wound healing.

The important role of macrophages for normal wound healing has been demonstrated in a number of empirical studies (Devalaraja et al., 2000; Ishida, Gao, & Murphy, 2008; Leibovich & Ross, 1975; Lucas et al., 2010; Mirza, DiPietro, & Koh, 2009). Over 30 years ago, Leibovich and Ross (1975) provided evidence using a guinea pig wound model that macrophage destruction in the wound area induced by an antiserum resulted in significantly delayed wound healing. The removal of dead neutrophils (an essential task of macrophages) from the wound area was reduced and the start and the extent of the proliferation of fibroblasts was delayed or reduced. These findings have also been confirmed by more recent studies using knock-out mice. Reduced infiltration of inflammatory monocytes as a result of reduced expression of adhesion molecules was associated with a delay in wound closure (Mori, Kondo, Nishie, Ohshima, & Asano, 2004; Nagaoka et al., 2000; Subramaniam et al., 1997). In addition, the group led by Lucas were recently able to verify that macrophages play different roles at different times during wound healing using targeted macrophage destruction in different phases of wound healing in a mouse model (Lucas et al., 2010). The destruction of macrophages during the inflammatory phase resulted in significantly reduced formation of vascularized granulation tissue and epithelial tissue. Macrophage destruction during the tissue formation phase is associated with severe hemorrhaging in wound tissue. On the other hand, destruction of macrophages in later phases of wound healing had no effect.

As the elimination of potential microbes, foreign particles and cell debris is paramount in the inflammatory phase of wound healing, it is likely that macrophages of the M1 phenotype are particularly relevant in this phase. In later phases, however, such as during the proliferation and remodeling phase, it appears to be the case that macrophages corresponding to the M2 phenotype are in demand. In fact, the group led by Daley was able to demonstrate using a mouse model of wound healing that one day after wound application, 85% of the macrophages had an M1 phenotype, but only 20% did so seven days after wounding (Daley, Brancato, Thomay, Reichner, & Albina, 2010). Moreover, according to Lucas and colleagues, five days after the injury, a macrophage similar to the M2 phenotype dominates the wound area (Lucas et al., 2010).

It is also assumed that in the course of the wound healing process, M1 macrophages are converted to M2 macrophages, whereby the latter seem to be partly responsible for the termination of the inflammatory phase. This switch from M1 to M2 macrophages might be triggered by phagocytosis of apoptotic cells (e.g., neutrophils; Duffield, 2003; Stout, 2010). A change in the cytokine environment in the wound area could also trigger a conversion of the M1 to the M2 phenotype (Khallou-Laschet et al., 2010). This hypothesis is supported by findings from *in vitro* studies which indicate that macrophage activation is plastic (see section 2.1.1.2.3; Stout et al., 2005; Stout & Suttles, 2004).

It must be pointed out here that in light of findings by McDonald and colleagues, the significance of macrophages in wound healing must be attributed to newly recruited macrophages rather than tissue-resident macrophages. The group was able to show that the destruction of tissue-resident macrophages neither delayed nor affected the efficiency of wound healing in mice (MacDonald et al., 2010).

2.4.3 Influence of psychological stress on wound healing

It has repeatedly been shown that both acute and chronic psychological stress slows wound healing in humans (for review see Walburn et al., 2009 or Gouin & Kiecolt-Glaser, 2011). For example, Robles found a delayed skin barrier recovery of 10% two hours after skin disruption (tape stripping) in subjects exposed to an acute stressor (TSST; Robles, 2007). In line with this, recovery of the skin barrier function after tape stripping was delayed by an acute stressor (TSST; Altemus et al., 2001). In another study, the wound healing was slowed by about 60% in couples with hostile marital interaction. This stress effect was associated with a reduced concentration of pro-inflammatory cytokines IL-1β, IL-6 and TNF-α in the wound area (Kiecolt-Glaser et al., 2005). A similar result was reported by Glaser and colleagues, who found that the cytokines IL-1α and IL-8 were negatively correlated with psychological stress (Glaser et al., 1999). Another study revealed that women who suffered from caregiving stress showed a significantly prolonged wound-healing process as compared to a control group (48 vs. 39 days). This slowed wound healing *in vivo* was also associated with reduced expression of the IL-1-gene in PBMC after LPS stimulation *in vitro* (Kiecolt-Glaser, Marucha, Malarkey, Mercado, & Glaser, 1995). Moreover, a more recent study showed that examination stress is associated with an overall suppressed neutrophil transcriptome in wound fluid (Roy et al., 2005). Taken together, the majority of these results indicate that the stress-induced, delayed wound healing is associated with a suppressed immune reaction during the inflammatory phase.

Regarding the mechanism by which stress prolongs wound healing time, an involvement of GC is speculated. In animal studies, several groups of authors provided empirical evidence that psychological stress (e.g. restraint stress) induced delayed wound healing, largely caused by GC (Denda, Tsuchiya, Elias, & Feingold, 2000; Kao et al., 2003; Padgett, Marucha, & Sheridan, 1998; Rojas et al., 2002). GC which were injected into mice delayed wound healing. Moreover, the application of the GC antagonist RU486 largely normalized the wound healing process (Denda et al., 2000; Kao et al., 2003;

Padgett et al., 1998; Rojas et al., 2002). More recently, there has been accumulating evidence that wound healing delays are mediated by SNS or released CA (Pullar, Grahn, Liu, & Isseroff, 2006; Pullar, Rizzo, & Isseroff, 2006; Sivamani et al., 2009). For example, Pullar and colleagues found a beta2-AR-mediated delay in re-epithelialization and a decrease in wound-induced epidermal ERK phosphorylation in human skin wounds (Pullar, Grahn et al., 2006). Furthermore, the authors demonstrated a beta2-AR-mediated delay in re-epithelialization in murine tail-clip wounds. However, the exact mechanisms by which stress prolongs wound healing time remain to be elucidated.

2.4.4 Summary

In vitro studies have demonstrated that inflammatory and microbicidal potential of human macrophages is primarily reduced by the stress hormones NE and EPI transmitted over beta 2 adrenergic receptors. Moreover, GC predominantly have an anti-inflammatory effect on monocytes / macrophages, although the profile of GC is modulated by various factors and is therefore difficult to predict.

The influence of psychological stress on the microbicidal potential of human macrophages has not been investigated in human studies, and only sporadically in animal studies. In contrast, there are numerous findings which emphasize the importance of macrophages for normal wound healing processes. Similarly, it is also well established that psychological stress delays wound healing. The mechanisms underlying this effect are currently being elucidated.

2.5 Conclusion, aims of the study and hypothesis

The above-discussed findings point towards the evidence that psychological stress may exert at least parts of its wound healing impairment by inhibiting the microbicidal potential and thus the microbicidal activity of newly recruited human M1 macrophages.

Although the effect of acute psychological stress on the microbicidal potential of M1 macrophages has not yet been investigated, a large body of research indicates that acute stress may influence M1 microbicidal potential by activating the HPA axis and / or the SNS. For example, macrophages express receptors for many neuroendocrine products of the HPA axis and the SNS, including receptors for GC, NE and EPI (Blotta, DeKruyff, & Umetsu, 1997; Reyes-Garcia & Garcia-Tamayo, 2009). Furthermore, macrophages play a significant role in skin wound healing (Mahdavian Delavary et al., 2011). In the inflammatory phase of wound healing, beginning about 1 hour after injury, the removal of potential microbes, foreign particles and cell debris is paramount. Recent studies indicate that these tasks are performed approximately 48 hours post-injury, primarily by newly recruited M1 macrophages characterized by high microbicidal activity (Daley et al., 2010; Engelhardt et al., 1998). Tissue-resident macrophages, in comparison, play a negligible role during this phase of wound healing (MacDonald et al., 2010).

On the other hand, it has been repeatedly shown that both acute and chronic psychological stress delays skin wound healing (Gouin & Kiecolt-Glaser, 2011). Human and animal studies indicate that this delayed skin wound healing is associated with a suppressed immune response in the wound area during the inflammatory phase. Furthermore, GC, NE and EPI appear to be involved in the stress-induced delay in wound healing (Denda, Tsuchiya, Elias, & Feingold, 2000; Kao et al., 2003; Padgett, Marucha, & Sheridan, 1998;

Pullar, Grahn et al., 2006). However, the exact mechanisms by which psychological stress delays wound healing in humans remain to be fully elucidated (Gouin & Kiecolt-Glaser, 2011).

Therefore, in order to shed more light on the mechanisms by which psychological stress delays skin wound healing, we aimed to investigate the effects of an acute psychological stressor on the microbicidal potential of newly recruited human M1 macrophages within a wound paradigm. We hypothesized that acute psychological stress would inhibit the microbicidal potential of newly recruited M1 macrophages. Furthermore, we examined whether the hypothesized inhibiting effect of psychological stress is mediated by the stress hormones NE, EPI and / or cortisol.

To the best of our knowledge, there were no simple and cost-efficient methods for analyzing the NADPH-mediated microbicidal potential of newly recruited human M1 macrophages. Thus, prior to the investigation of the essential research question, an appropriate method had to be established. Consequently, the first aim of this thesis was to implement and validate a simple and cost-efficient *in vitro* method suitable for assessing the NADPH-mediated microbicidal potential of classically activated monocyte-derived human macrophages.

3 Empirical studies

In the following, the two studies underlying this thesis are presented consecutively: first, the implementation study, and subsequently, the stress study.

3.1 A simple in vitro method to investigate the microbicidal potential of human macrophages

3.1.1 Introduction

A growing body of psychoneuroimmunological research documents that psychological states are linked to quantitative und qualitative alterations in circulating leukocytes (e.g. Ader, 2006; Rabin, 1999). In contrast, relatively little is known about associations between psychological states and alterations in leukocytes in peripheral tissues such as tissue-based macrophages. However, classically activated M1 macrophages are important effector cells involved in warding off microbes and in the first phase of wound healing – both known to be associated with psychological states (Adams, 1994; Glaser, 2005; Glaser & Kiecolt-Glaser, 2005; Gouin & Kiecolt-Glaser, 2011; P. R. Taylor et al., 2005).

The lack of research in the field of PNI may be related to both the absence of and familiarity with simple and cost-efficient methods of analyzing the activity of human M1 macrophages. Given that M1 macrophages are primarily activated to develop microbicidal effector functions (Schroder et al., 2004), the objective of this study was to implement a simple, cost-effective and valid *in vitro* method to investigate microbicidal potential of *ex vivo* isolated HMDM.

The method presented here is the WST-1 macrophage assay, an *in vitro* assay we previously applied successfully in THP-1 cells (Sakai et al., 2009). The WST-1 macrophage assay principle is based on the fact that the microbicidal potential of human macrophages is highly dependent on the generation of pathogen-killing ROS, a process termed oxidative burst (Babior, 1984, 2000; H. W. Murray & Cohn, 1980). More specifically, the oxidative burst is characterized by a stimulus-induced sharp increase in oxygen consumption and the activation of a plasma membrane-bound enzyme complex called NADPH oxidase (El-Benna et al., 2005). Activated NADPH oxidase catalyzes the one-electron reduction of oxygen to O_2^- which in turn reduces WST-1, a cell-impermeative tetrazolium salt (Sakai et al., 2009; Tan & Berridge, 2000). The reduction of WST-1 results in the formation of a colored, water-soluble formazan salt with increased absorbance at 450 nm (Sakai et al., 2009; Tan & Berridge, 2000).

Consequently, the colorimetric measurement of formazan formation in the medium in which macrophages are suspended is a precise indicator of superoxide anion-induced WST-1 reduction and thus of macrophage microbicidal potential.

The purpose of this study was to implement and validate a simple, cost-efficient *in vitro* method suitable for assessing microbicidal potential of *ex vivo* isolated HMDM which may be used in future psychoneuroimmunological research.

3.1.2 Materials and methods

3.1.2.1 Reagents and chemicals

We used the following reagents: Ficoll-Paque PLUS (Ficoll; no. 17-1440-02; GE Healthcare; Uppsala, Sweden); WST-1 (no. 150849-52-8, Dojindo Laboratories;

Kumamoto, Japan); IFN-γ (no. PHC4031, Invitrogen; Basel, Switzerland), TNF-α; (no. PHC3016, Invitrogen; Basel, Switzerland); Hank's balanced salt solution without phenol red (HBSS; no. 14025050, Invitrogen; Basel, Switzerland); fetal bovine serum (FBS; no. 10106-169, Invitrogen; Basel, Switzerland); LPS (no.L6529, Sigma-Aldrich; Buchs, Switzerland); phosphate buffered saline (PBS; no. P5368, Sigma-Aldrich; Buchs, Switzerland); phorbol 12-myristate 13-acetate (PMA; no. P8139, Sigma-Aldrich; Buchs, Switzerland); dimethyl sulfoxide (DMSO; no. D2650, Sigma-Aldrich; Buchs, Switzerland); RPMI-1640 Media with Glutamax (RPMI-1640; no. W9925E, Fisher Scientifc; Wohlen, Switzerland).

3.1.2.2 Participants and procedure

Study participants for assay implementation and validation by current generation were 21 healthy, medication-free, non-smoking Caucasian men with a mean age of 35.0 years (SEM = 2.32, range = 20-50 years) and a mean BMI of 24.7 kg/m^2 (SEM = 0.76, range = 18.7-33.2 kg/m^2). Participants were recruited via advertisements and with the help of the Swiss Red Cross of the canton of Zurich. Each participant provided a blood sample taken at approximately 1:30 p.m. The study protocol was formally approved by the Ethics Committee of the canton of Zurich, Switzerland, and written informed consent was obtained from all subjects.

3.1.2.3 The WST-1 macrophage assay, an in vitro method for assessing macrophage microbicidal potential

The method used in this study to measure macrophage O_2^- production is an adaption of a method used in a permanent THP-1 cells as described by Sakai et al. (2009).

3.1.2.3.1 Isolation of peripheral blood nuclear cells

Nine milliliters of blood were collected in ethylenediaminetetraacetic acid (EDTA)-coated tubes (Sarstedt, Numbrecht, Germany) and immediately centrifuged for 10 minutes at 2000 g and 4°C. The plasma supernatant was removed and stored at -80°C for further analyses not relevant to this study. The remaining cell pellet was re-suspended in 3 ml 0.01 M PBS (pH 7.4). This cell suspension was layered on top of 10 ml Ficoll and centrifuged for 20 minutes at 300 g and 20°C. After centrifugation, PBMC were removed from the interface, washed twice in RPMI1640 medium, counted with a hematologic analyzer (KX-21N; Sysmex Digitana AG), and re-suspended to a concentration of 2.5 x 10^6/ml with RPMI-1640 with 10% FBS.

3.1.2.3.2 Differentiation of human monocytes into macrophages and their separation

PBMC suspension aliquots of 1 ml were transferred to 24-well cell culture plates (no. 4609; Semadeni; Ostermundigen, Switzerland). We added 0.5 µl LPS, 5 µl IFN-γ, and 2 µl TNF-α resulting in a final concentration of 300 ng/ml LPS, 50 ng/ml IFN-γ, and 20 ng/ml TNF-α to promote differentiation of monocytes into macrophages as well as to prime cells for enhanced PMA-stimulated O_2^- release. After incubation for 48 h at 37°C and 5% CO_2, the plate surface was rinsed three times with 1 ml of warm (25°C) 0.01 M PBS to remove non-adherent PBMC, while HMDM remained adherent to the bottom of the plates.

3.1.2.3.3 WST-1 assay to determine superoxide anion production

Next, the resulting macrophage monolayer (obtained as described above) was overlaid with 1 ml HBSS. Subsequently, 2 µl WST-1, 0.5 µl LPS, 5 µl IFN-γ, 2 µl TNF-α, and 0,5 µl PMA were added, resulting in a final concentration of 100 µM WST-1, 300 ng/ml LPS, 50 ng/ml IFN-γ, 20 ng/ml TNF-α, and 50 nM PMA. This was followed by an incubation period of 4 hours at 37°C and 5% CO_2. Then, the supernatant was removed and used to determine WST-1 reduction by reading the OD with a spectrophotometer (SmartSpec Plus, Bio-Rad Laboratories, Inc.) at 450 nm against water as blank. Increases in absorbance are proportional to the amount of WST-1 reduced or O_2^- generated by HMDM, respectively.

3.1.2.4 Assay implementation and validation procedures

3.1.2.4.1 Identification and verification of macrophage superoxide anion production stimulating agents

In order to verify the applicability of the cell-line tested *in vitro* method for *ex vivo* isolated HMDM, we tested the influence of different stimuli on the O_2^- production of *ex vivo* isolated human monocytes. Following Sakai and colleagues (2009), we used stimuli which initiate either cell differentiation, cell activation or both cell differentiation and activation. For cell differentiation we used the combination of LPS, IFN-γ, and TNF-α; for cell activation we used PMA. Combined differentiation and activation included the use of LPS, IFN-γ, TNF-α, and PMA (detailed protocol in section 3.1.2.3). All stimulation experiments were repeated three times and carried out in cells of one female subject.

3.1.2.4.2 Validation of macrophage superoxide anion production by generation of electrical current

Current generation observed in the biofuel cell developed by Sakai et al. (2009) primarily originates from PMA-induced O_2^- release by THP-1-derived macrophages. The greater the O_2^- release, the greater the current generation. Therefore, the quantity of electrical power produced in this biofuel cell setup represents a suitable criterion for the validation of the WST-1 macrophage assay.

The biofuel cell was constructed and operated as described by Sakai et al. (2009). Briefly, 2.5 x 10^6 PBMC/ml were isolated as described in section 3.1.2.3.1. Then, PBMC suspension aliquots of 3 ml were seeded on a gold electrode in custom-made incubation containers. For cell differentiation, we added 1.5 µl LPS, 15 µl IFN-γ, and 6 µl TNF-α resulting in equivalent final concentrations as for the WST-1 macrophage assay (300 ng/ml LPS, 20 ng/ml IFN-γ, and 20 ng/ml TNF-α; see section 3.1.2.3.2). During a 48h incubation period at 37°C and 5% CO_2, HMDM became adherent to the electrode. After incubation, the electrode with HMDM was transferred to the anode compartment of a custom-made two-compartment biofuel cell. While the anode compartment was filled with 6 ml HBSS containing 300 ng/ml LPS, 20 ng/ml IFN-γ, and 20 ng/ml TNF-α, the fluid in the cathode compartment was HBSS with 0.1M potassium ferricyanide. For current generation, we added 3 µl PMA to the anode compartment corresponding to a concentration of 50 nM PMA. The PMA-induced current (µ Ampere, µA) was calculated from the voltage drop measured across a resistor with a digital multimeter (2000, Keithley Instruments Inc.). Current production was recorded continuously for four hours.

3.1.2.5 Statistical analysis

Data were analyzed using SPSS Inc. version 17.0 for Windows (Statistical Package for the Social Sciences, SPSS, Chicago, IL, USA) and presented as mean $\pm$ *SEM*. All tests were 2-tailed with the level of significance set at $p < .05$.

Since current generation was monitored continuously, we extracted two indices to reflect power generation from the four-hour recording period: first the maximum current value registered (C_{Max}) and then the sum of all current values (C_{Sum}).

Pearson correlations were used to validate O_2^- induced macrophage WST-1 reduction by O_2^- induced macrophage current generation.

3.1.3 Results

3.1.3.1 Identification and verification of macrophage superoxide anion production stimulating agents

Figure 6 illustrates that *ex vivo* isolated human monocytes exposed to both differentiation and activation stimuli showed the greatest WST-1 reduction (1.2 ± 0.2). In contrast, cells treated with the activator PMA (0.09 ± 0.04) or with differentiation stimuli (0.03 ± 0.003) only revealed low WST-1 reduction capacity. As expected, non-stimulated cells showed the lowest amounts of reduced WST-1 (0.02 ± 0.01; negative control). The amount of reduced WST-1 reflects O_2^- production by the cells and thus macrophage microbicidal potential. These results indicate that stimulation by combined cell differentiating and activating agents constitutes the most effective procedure for inducing O_2^- responses.

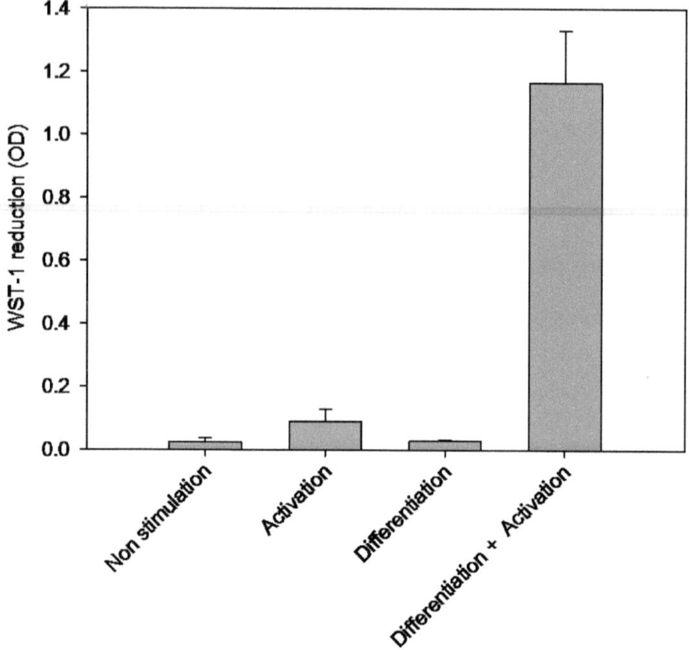

Figure 6. WST-1 reduction by *ex vivo* isolated human monocyte-derived macrophages after differential stimulation. From the left: Untreated cells as negative control; activation with 50 nM PMA; differentiation with 300 ng/ml LPS, 50 ng/ml IFN-γ, and 20 ng/ml TNF-α; differentiation and activation stimuli (300 ng/ml LPS, 50 ng/ml IFN-γ, 20 ng/ml TNF-α, 50 nM PMA). Values are given as mean ± *SEM,* triple determination.

3.1.3.2 WST-1 macrophage assay implementation results

WST-1 reduction scores ($n = 21$) are depicted in Figure 7 and Figure 8. The WST-1 macrophage assay induced O_2^- responses by HMDM (as reflected by WST-1 reduction ODs) in all subjects (0.29 ± 0.02, range: $0.12 - 0.47$ OD).

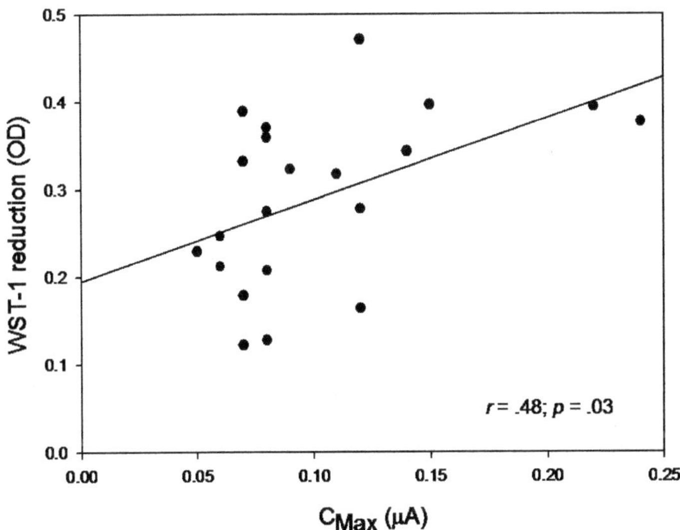

Figure 7. Scatter plot of the maximum current value registered (C$_{Max}$) and WST-1 reduction.

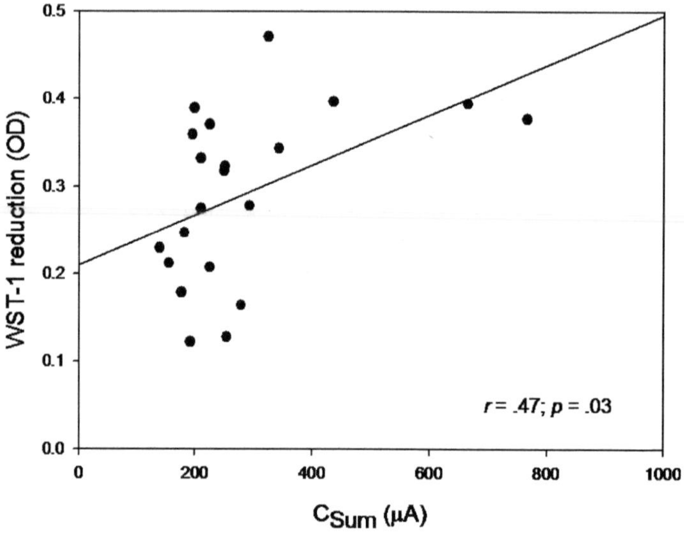

Figure 8. Scatter plot of the sum of all current values (C_{Sum}) and WST-1 reduction.

3.1.3.3 Assay validation by current generation

We observed current generation in HMDM of all subjects (C_{Max} = 0.10 ± 0.01 µA, range = 0.05-0.24 µA; C_{Sum} = 284.12 ± 34.83 µA, range = 139.01-765.77 µA). Higher WST-1 reduction scores correlated significantly with higher current generation (r (WST-1 reduction / C_{Max}) = .48; p = .03; Figure 7); r (WST-1 reduction / C_{Sum}) = .47; p = .03; Figure 8).

3.1.4 Discussion

In this study, we implemented and validated a cost-efficient and simple *in vitro* method which allows to investigate the NADPH oxidase-mediated microbicidal potential of *ex vivo* isolated HMDM.

In order to implement the WST-1 macrophage assay, we examined applicability of the cell-line tested *in vitro* method for *ex vivo* isolated HMDM. Similar to THP-1 cells (Sakai et al., 2009), *ex vivo* isolated human monocytes exposed to both differentiating and activating agents produced the greatest amounts of O_2^- compared to cells treated with either differentiating or activating stimuli alone. Application of the WST-1 macrophage assay in a larger sample evoked significant PMA-induced O_2^- responses by HMDM in all subjects. These findings indicate that the *in vitro* method described for THP-1 cells is applicable to *ex vivo* isolated HMDM. Furthermore, we evaluated the validity of the assay by comparing WST-1 reduction scores with electricity scores and found that greater WST-1 reduction was associated with greater current generation. Given that current production in the fuel cell only partially originates from O_2^- produced by HMDM, while the level of WST-1 reduction is almost completely based on HMDM O_2^- release, the observed moderate height of the correlation coefficients in our study (r (WST-1 reduction / C_{Max}) = .48; r (WST-1 reduction / C_{Sum}) = .47) suggests that the WST-1 macrophage assay provides a valid assessment of O_2^- production by HMDM.

There are several potential implications for the implementation of the WST-1 macrophage assay. Thus far in the study of psychoneuroimmunology, there has been a lack not only of simple and cost-efficient methods for investigating microbicidal potential of human macrophages but also of literature regarding their associations to psychological states.

However, elucidating the relationship between psychological states and microbicidal potential of macrophages may contribute to a better understanding of the biological mechanisms linking psychological risk factors with adverse health consequences (e.g. increased susceptibility to infectious diseases, or impaired wound healing) where classically activated macrophages and thus peripheral leukocyte activity play a major role (Ross, 1999; Rozanski, Blumenthal, Davidson, Saab, & Kubzansky, 2005). The WST-1 macrophage assay may facilitate future research in this important field.

The present study has two limitations. First, we did not further determine the sensitivity limit of the method. In other words, we did not establish the lowest cell concentration of PBMC needed to still enable the measurement of PMA-induced O_2^- release by HMDM. However, based on our experience, the cell concentration used should be higher than 1.8 x 10^6 PBMC / ml. Second, the stability and thus reliability of the measurements of subjects over time requires further investigation. Notably, the consistently low *SEM* values of the repeated stimulation experiments (three repetitions of four different stimulation conditions in cells of one female subject with blood drawn on three different days) suggest high reproducibility of assay results over time.

The WST-macrophage assay has several strengths. First, the *in vitro* method implemented requires no expensive laboratory equipment or reagents, nor does it involve complicated and time-consuming procedures. In contrast, one alternative method, the O_2^- induced current generation, is less advantageous since it requires non-commercially available equipment and there may be sample loss during the preparation procedure of very sensitive materials such as the gold-coated glass electrodes. Second, the WST-1 assay allows a more precise assessment of NADPH oxidase-mediated microbicidal macrophage potential since the level of WST-1 reduction results almost entirely from HMDM O_2^-

release, whereas current production in the fuel cell originates only partially from O_2^- produced by HMDM (Sakai et al., 2009).

In summary, our data suggest that we successfully implemented a simple and cost-efficient *in vitro* method allowing valid investigation of NADPH oxidase-mediated microbicidal potential of *ex vivo* isolated HMDM and thus of peripheral leukocyte activity.

3.2 Acute stress reduces microbicidal potential of *ex vivo* isolated human monocyte-derived macrophages

3.2.1 Introduction

Psychological stress induces pronounced changes in both innate and adaptive immune cell responses that can induce adverse health consequences such as increased susceptibility to infectious diseases and impaired wound healing (Irwin, 2008; Yang & Glaser, 2002). Whereas effects of acute psychological stress on blood leukocytes as circulating immune cells have been well documented (Dragos & Tanasescu, 2010), comparatively little is known about stress reactivity of leukocytes in peripheral tissues.

Macrophages are tissue-based leukocytes that are differentiated from circulating blood monocytes. When activated, macrophages acquire competence to perform a variety of critical immunological functions, including the killing of microbes (i.e. microbicidal activity) and tumor cells, regulation of lymphocytes and inflammation, or remodeling and repair of tissue (Schroder et al., 2004; Taylor et al., 2005; Woods, 2000). In particular, macrophage microbicidal activity plays a significant role in early phases of inflammation such as the first phases of skin wound healing (Mahdavian Delavary et al., 2011). Macrophage activation in terms of microbicidal activity can be investigated in pro-inflammatory M1 macrophages. The M1 macrophage is a phenotype developed following activation with inflammatory cytokines (e.g. IFN-γ, TNF-α) and bacterial products (e.g. LPS; Pelegrin & Surprenant, 2009; Taylor et al., 2005). M1 macrophages are characterized by enhanced microbicidal activity (Hunter et al., 2009; Martinez et al., 2008), mainly mediated by increased secretion of microbe killing, highly oxidizing agents, the so-called ROS (e.g. O_2^-, H_2O_2) and RNS (e.g. NO; Dale et al., 2008; Taylor et al., 2005). Moreover, these cells secrete high amounts of chemokines and pro-inflammatory cytokines (Taylor et al., 2005).

Given that psychological stress can impair wound healing (Altemus et al., 2001; Robles, 2007; Robles et al., 2009; Walburn et al., 2009), and given the role of microbicidally active M1 macrophages in early wound healing phases (Mahdavian Delavary et al., 2011), it might be speculated that stress may exert at least parts of its wound healing impairment by inhibiting M1 microbicidal potential – the precondition for microbicidal activity. However, the effect of acute psychological stress on the microbicidal potential of human M1 macrophages has not yet been investigated. In line with the previous reasoning, acute stress may influence M1 microbicidal potential via activation of the HPA axis and / or the SNS. Both monocytes and macrophages express receptors for a variety of neuroendocrine products of the HPA axis and the SNS (e.g. receptors for GC and CA; Blotta et al., 1997; Reyes-Garcia & Garcia-Tamayo, 2009; Rouppe van der Voort et al., 2000; Woods, 2000). Moreover, *in vitro* studies exposing monocytes and macrophages to GC or CA demonstrated predominantly hormone-induced decreases in microbicidal potential (Ehrchen et al., 2007; Ortega et al., 2000; Reyes-Garcia & Garcia-Tamayo, 2009;

Stanojevic et al., 2007) Similarly, studies in rodents investigating the effects of psychological stress on the microbicidal potential of *ex vivo* isolated tissue-resident macrophages reported stress-induced, albeit inconsistent changes in production of ROS and RNS (Palermo-Neto et al., 2003; Persoons et al., 1997; Stanojevic et al., 2007). Thus, stress-induced release of GC as the final products of the HPA axis activation and of the CA release may modulate macrophage microbicidal potential.

The purpose of this study was twofold: First, in a sample of healthy men, we examined the effects of a potent acute psychological stressor known to induce large stress hormone increases compared to a non-stress control condition on microbicidal potential of M1 macrophages. To stimulate circulating monocytes as precursors of later M1 macrophages *in vivo*, we applied an open wound by insertion of a venous catheter. Stress was induced in half of the sample via the widely used TSST (Kirschbaum et al., 1993). For the investigation of M1 cell microbicidal potential, we used the WST-1 macrophage assay as recently developed and implemented by our group (Kuebler et al., submitted; for details see section 3.1). The assay principle is based on the reduction of WST-1 by superoxide anions produced by PMA-activated human monocyte-derived M1 macrophages (HMDM). We hypothesized that acute psychological stress would inhibit microbicidal potential of HMDM. Second, in order to investigate underlying mechanisms, we tested whether the hypothesized inhibiting effect of stress is statistically mediated by blood NE, EPI and / or cortisol levels.

3.2.2 Methods and materials

3.2.2.1 Participants

The Ethics Committee of the Canton of Zurich, Switzerland formally approved the research protocol. Subjects were recruited with the aid of the Swiss Red Cross of the Canton of Zurich and through advertisements. All subjects gave written informed consent before participating in the study.

For the purpose of the present study, we intentionally recruited 44 medication-free, healthy Caucasian men between 20 and 50 yrs of age and obtained complete WST-1 reduction data from 41 of these subjects. Subjects were randomly assigned to either a stress ($n = 24$) or a control group ($n = 20$). Three control group subjects had to be excluded due to venous catheter occlusion. Table 2 provides characteristics of the stress group ($n = 24$) and the final control group ($n = 17$). Subjects were in good physical and mental health, as confirmed by a telephone interview. Explicit exclusion criteria were: regular strenuous exercise, smoking, alcohol and illicit drug abuse, any heart disease, varicosis or thrombotic diseases, elevated blood sugar and diabetes, elevated cholesterol, liver and renal diseases, chronic obstructive pulmonary disease, allergies and atopic diathesis, rheumatic diseases, and current infectious diseases. If the personal or medication history was not conclusive, the subjects' primary care physician was contacted for verification.

3.2.2.2 Experimental protocol

All subjects reported to the laboratory by 10 a.m. and had abstained from extensive physical exercise, alcohol, and caffeinated beverages during the previous 24 h. Subjects were given a calorically standardized breakfast with comparable nutritional composition before an indwelling venous catheter was inserted not only for blood sampling but also to induce an open wound. The following resting period of 165 min was intended to allow *in vivo* stimulation of circulating monocytes by the applied open wound paradigm. Next, subjects of the stress group were exposed to the TSST (Kirschbaum et al., 1993), which comprises a short introduction followed by a 5-min preparation period, a 5-min mock job interview, and a 5-min mental arithmetic task (serial subtraction) in front of an unknown panel of two persons. The TSST has repeatedly been shown to induce significant neuroendocrine stress responses (Dickerson & Kemeny, 2004). Subjects of the control group were not exposed to the TSST but were required to stand in the empty TSST room for 10 minutes in order to control for a possible influence of orthostatic stress. Before and after TSST / rest, subjects remained seated in a quiet room.

Blood samples for WST-1 reduction measurements were obtained immediately before (serving as baseline levels) and after TSST / rest, as well as 10 and 60 min after TSST / rest cessation. To determine CA levels, blood samples were taken immediately before (baseline) and after, in addition to 10, and 20 min after TSST / rest cessation. For determination of salivary free cortisol levels, samples of saliva were collected immediately before (baseline) and after, and 10, 20, 30, 45, and 60 min after TSST / rest cessation. To determine mean arterial blood pressure (MAP), blood pressure was measured by sphygmomanometry (Omron 773, Omron Healthcare Europe B.V. Hoofdorp, Netherlands) immediately before and 40 min after insertion of the venous catheter. MAP was calculated by the formula (2/3 * mean diastolic BP) + (1/3 mean systolic BP). At the end of the experiment, participants were debriefed and remunerated with 175 Swiss Francs for their participation.

3.2.2.3 WST-1 macrophage assay

The method used to study microbicidal potential of *ex vivo* isolated HMDM is based on that described by Kuebler et al. (submitted). In brief, 9 ml of blood were collected in EDTA-coated tubes (Sarstedt, Numbrecht, Germany) and immediately centrifuged for 10 minutes at 2000 g and 4°C. The plasma supernatant was removed and stored at -80°C for further analyses not relevant to this study. The remaining cell pellet was re-suspended in 3 ml 0.01 M PBS (pH 7.4). This cell suspension was layered on top of 10 ml Ficoll and centrifuged for 20 minutes at 300 g and 20°C. After centrifugation, PBMC were removed from the interface, washed twice in RPMI1640 medium, counted with a hematologic analyzer (KX-21N; Sysmex Digitana AG), and re-suspended to a concentration of 2.5 x 10^6/ml with RPMI-1640 with 10% FBS.

1 ml of this PBMC suspension was transferred to 24-well cell culture plates (no. 4609; Semadeni [Ostermundingen, Schweiz]). Then, we added 5 µl IFN-γ, 2 µl TNF-α, and 0.5 µl LPS, resulting in a final concentration of 50 ng/ml IFN-γ, 20 ng/ml TNF-α, and 300 ng/ml LPS to promote differentiation of monocytes into M1 macrophages as well as to prime cells for enhanced PMA-stimulated O_2^- release. After incubation for 48 h at 37°C and 5% CO_2, the plate surface was rinsed three times with 1 ml of warm (25°C) 0.01 M PBS to remove non-adherent PBMC, while HMDM remained adherent to the bottom of the plates.

Next, the resulting macrophage monolayer (obtained as described above) was overlaid with 1 ml HBSS. Subsequently, 2 µl WST-1, 0.5 µl LPS, 5 µl IFN-γ, 2 µl TNF-α, and 0,5 µl PMA were added, resulting in a final concentration of 100 µM WST-1, 300 ng/ml LPS, 50 ng/ml IFN-γ, 20 ng/ml TNF-α, and 50 nM PMA. This was followed by an incubation period of 4 hours at 37°C and 5% CO_2. Then, the supernatant was removed and used to determine WST-1 reduction by reading the OD with a spectrophotometer (SmartSpec Plus, Bio-Rad Laboratories, Inc.) at 450 nm against water as blank. Increases in absorbance are proportional to the amount of WST-1 reduced or O_2^- generated by HMDM, respectively.

3.2.2.4 Stress hormone assays

For CA assessment, venous blood was drawn in EDTA-coated monovettes (Sarstedt, Numbrecht, Germany), and immediately centrifuged for 10 minutes at 2000 x g and 4°C. Obtained plasma was stored at -80°C until analysis. Plasma catecholamine levels were determined by means of high-pressure liquid chromatography (HPLC) and electrochemical detection after liquid-liquid extraction (Ehrenreich et al., 1997; Smedes, Kraak, & Poppe, 1982) in the "Laboratory for Stress Monitoring" (Göttingen, Germany). For both NE and EPI, the detection limit was 6 pg/ml and inter- and intra-assay coefficients of variance (CVs) were < 5%.

For cortisol, saliva samples were collected in Salivettes (Sarstedt, Sevelen, Switzerland) and stored at -20°C until analysis. Centrifugation of thawed saliva samples was at 3000 x g, yielding low-viscosity saliva. Free cortisol concentrations were determined using a commercial chemiluminescence immunoassay (LIA) with high sensitivity of 0.16 ng/ml (IBL Hamburg, Germany). Inter- and intra CVs were <11.5% and 7.7%, respectively.

3.2.2.5 Statistical analysis

Data were analyzed using SPSS Inc. version 17.0 for Windows (Chicago, IL, USA) and presented as mean ± SEM. All tests were two-tailed with the significance level set at $p \leq$

0.05 and the level of borderline significance set at $p \leq 0.10$. Missing data were excluded listwise.

A priori sample size calculations were performed using G-power (Buchner et al., 1997). Based on previous observations (Atanackovic, Schulze, Kroger, Brunner-Weinzierl, & Deter, 2003), we expected a large effect size of 0.40 in terms of stress reactivity of HMDM. Statistical power analyses indicated that the optimal sample size to predict a large effect size of 0.40 in repeated measures analysis of covariance (ANCOVA; with HMDM as repeated factor) with a power of .90 is $n = 44$.

Prior to statistical analyses, data were tested for normal distribution and homogeneity of variance using Kolmogorov-Smirnov and Levene's tests. Skewed EPI values were logarithmically transformed and normal distribution was verified.

We determined stress hormone changes by calculating the difference between the expected peak stress response minus baseline level. NE and EPI changes (ΔNE; ΔEPI) were calculated as the difference in plasma levels between immediately post-TSST / rest and baseline. Cortisol stress changes (ΔCORT) refer to changes from baseline to 20 min post-TSST / rest. BMI was calculated by the formula weight in kg/(height in m)^2.

Differences between the characteristics of the two subject groups were calculated using univariate analysis of variance (ANOVA; Table 2).

To test whether the stressor evoked a significant neuroendocrine stress response, we calculated repeated measures ANOVAs with group (stress vs. control) as the independent variable and the 4 and 7 time points in which CA (NE and EPI) or cortisol were measured as repeated dependent variable.

In order to investigate stress reactivity of HMDM microbicidal potential, we calculated repeated measures ANCOVA with group as independent variable and the four WST-1 reduction time points (baseline, immediately-post TSST / rest, +10 min, and +60 min) as repeated dependent variable. Due to high levels of inter-individual variations, we followed previous research (Ellard, Castle, & Mian, 2001) and calculated percentage changes in WST-1 reduction at each of the time points after TSST / rest cessation in relation to baseline as indicators of stress-induced changes in HMDM microbicidal potential. Post-hoc testing of significant WST-1 reduction effects comprised (1) ANCOVAs to test for group differences in each measured WST-1 reduction time point, and (2) separate recalculation of repeated ANCOVAs in each subject group.

To test for a potential mediation of microbicidal potential by stress hormone release, we tested whether NE, EPI or cortisol changes (i.e. ΔNE, ΔEPI, ΔCORT) mediate the stress effect on microbicidal activity of HMDM. A statistical mediation holds if (step 1) the independent variable (group, i.e. stress vs. rest) is associated with the supposed mediator (i.e. NE, EPI, or cortisol stress increases), if (step 2) the independent variable (group) is associated with the dependent variable (repeated WST-1 reduction), and if (step 3) the mediator (i.e. NE, EPI, or cortisol changes) is significantly associated with the dependent variable (repeated WST-1 reduction) while controlling for the independent variable (i.e. group) and the association between the independent variable (group) and the dependent variable (WST-1 reduction) needs to be less than in step 2 (Baron and Kenny, 1986). Post-hoc testing of significant mediation effects comprised partial correlations between significant endocrine mediator variables and each WST-1 reduction time point.

We controlled for age, MAP, and BMI in all WST-1 reduction analyses as a priori selected control variables (i.e. covariates in ANCOVAs) based on previous literature suggesting a potential influence on microbicidal potential of HMDM (Dunston & Griffiths, 2010; Wirtz, Ehlert, Emini, & Suter, 2008; Wirtz, von Kanel, Frey, Ehlert, & Fischer, 2004).

Huynh-Feldt correction for repeated measures was applied where appropriate. Effect size parameters (f) were calculated from partial η^2-values and are reported where appropriate (effect size conventions: f: .10 = small, .25 = medium, .40 = large).

3.2.3 Results

3.2.3.1 Characteristics of the two subject groups

Table 2 provides the characteristics of the 24 stressed subjects and 17 controls studied. The two groups did not differ significantly in the proportion of age, BMI, MAP, NE, and EPI levels. Cortisol baseline levels were higher in the stress group than in control subjects. As expected, stressed subjects had higher stress hormone changes (ΔEPI; ΔNE; ΔCORT) than controls. Due to technical problems, NE data were missing in 2 subjects of the control group, and EPI data were missing in 4 subjects of the stress group, as well as in 2 subjects of the control group.

Table 2.

Characteristics of the 41 subjects studied

	Stress group ($n = 24$)	Control group ($n = 17$)	*P-* ANOVA
Age (yr)	35.9±1.9 (20-50)	34.7±1.9 (22-49)	.66
BMI (kg/m^2)	24.4±0.8 (18.7-36.0)	24.6± 0.5 (22.5-30.1)	.87
MAP (mm Hg)	89.6±1.8 (75.8-105.5)	87.8±1.3 (80.8-102.5)	.45
Stress hormone baseline levels			
NE (pg/ml)	448.5±38.2 (115.3-841.7)	419.2±48.5 (166.2-765.6)	.64
EPI (pg/ml)	22.6±3.8 (6.1-79.1)	20.9±3.5 (7.1-47.3)	.75
Cortisol (nmol/l)	5.3±0.5 (2.9-13.7)	3.7±0.4 (1.6-8.2)	.03
Stress hormone changes			
ΔNE (pg/ml)	239.5±24.7 (25.6-511.0)	64.1±23.0(-109.5-212.9)	<.001
ΔEPI (pg/ml)	43.4±9.2 (5.3-157.5)	4.5±2.3 (-13.9-20.2)	<.01
ΔCORT (nmol/l)	15.7±2.1 (-1.0-40.5)	0.7±0.8 (-1.6-12.3)	<.001

Notes. Values are given as means ± *SEM* (range). BMI, body mass index; MAP, mean arterial pressure; NE, norepinephrine; EPI, epinephrine.

3.2.3.2 Validation check of the neuroendocrine stress response

Stress induced significant increases in all stress hormones as compared to controls (NE: group x time interaction: $F(3,108) = 8.94$, $p<.001$; EPI: group x time interaction: $F(3, 90) = 15.35$, $p<.001$; cortisol: group x time interaction: $F(2.6, 98,5) = 25.6$, $p<.001$; Figures 9-11).

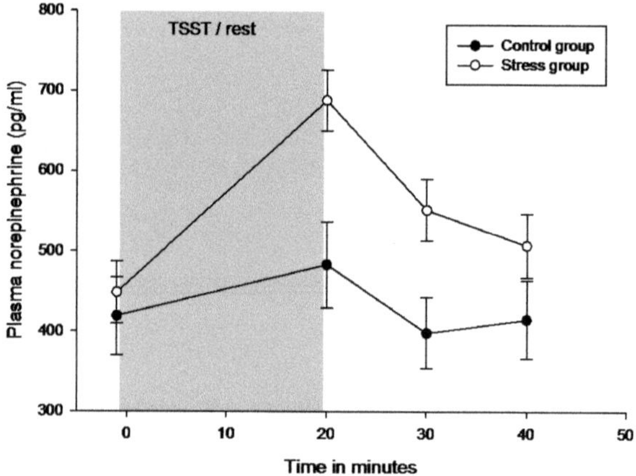

Figure 9. Course of norepinephrine over time in stress and control group. Values are given as means ± *SEM.*

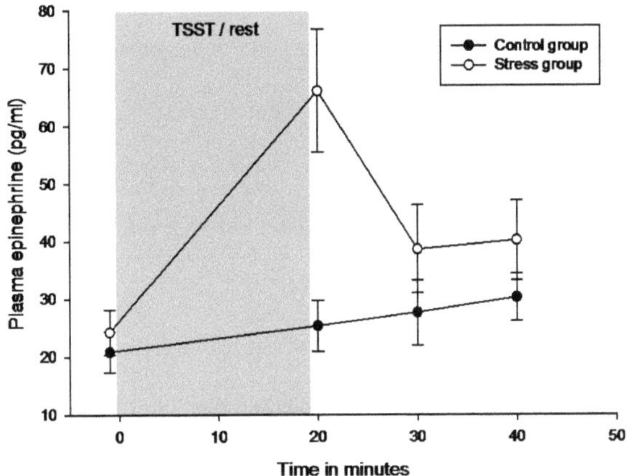

Figure 10. Course of epinephrine over time in stress and control group. Values are given as means ± *SEM.*

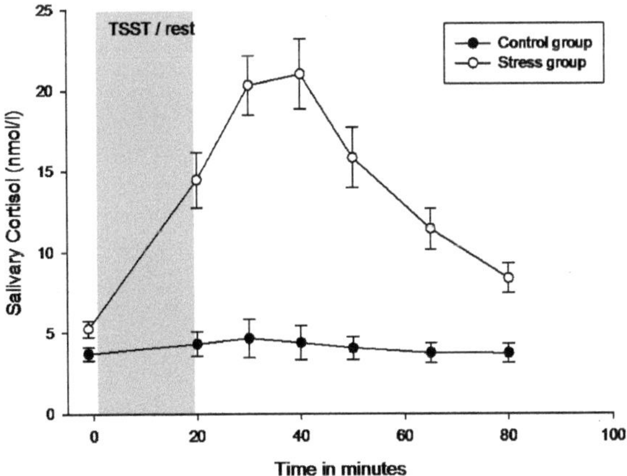

Figure 11. Course of cortisol over time in stress and control group. Values are given as means ± *SEM.*

3.2.3.3 Stress reactivity of WST-1 reduction by macrophages

Macrophage microbicidal potential in terms of WST-1 reduction was attenuated over time in the stress group as compared to the control group (main effect of group ($F(1/36) = 8.65$, $p = .01$), group x time interaction ($F(3/108) = 2.41$, $p = .07$; Figure 12). Post hoc testing revealed that stressed subjects had a significantly reduced WST-1 reduction immediately ($F(1, 36) = 8.9$, $p = .005$) and 10 min ($F(1, 36) = 4.1$, $p = .05$) after stress compared with controls. The difference between groups was of borderline significance 60 min after TSST / rest ($F(1, 36) = 3.6$, $p = 0.7$). Moreover, while the control group displayed a significant increase in WST-1 reduction over time ($F(3/39) = 3.83$, $p = .02$), the stress group did not ($F(3/60) = 0.30$, $p = .83$).

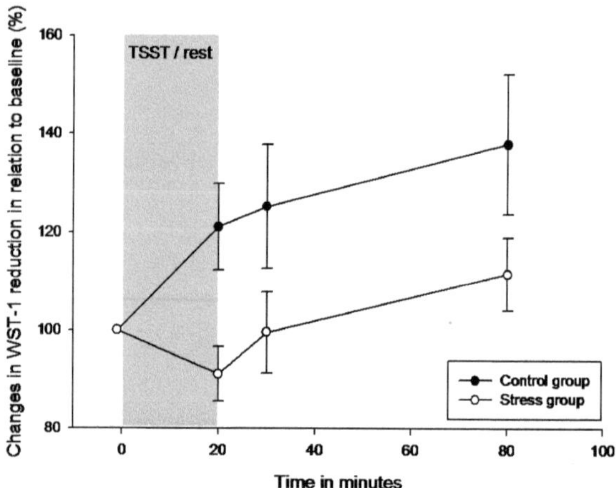

Figure 12. Course of WST-1 reduction over time in stress and control group. Values are given as means ± *SEM.*

3.2.3.4 Mediation of WST-1 reduction by stress hormone changes

Table 3 depicts partial correlations between WST-1 reduction measures and stress hormone change coefficients. Statistical mediation testing revealed that the change in NE significantly mediated the observed stress-induced attenuation of repeated macrophage microbicidal potential in terms of WST-1 reduction: (1) the group variable was significantly associated with ΔNE ($F(1/35) = 22.38$, $p<.001$, $\eta_p{}^2 = 0.39$) and (2) with repeated WST-1 reduction ($F (1/37) = 8.65$, $p =.005$, $\eta_p{}^2 = .19$). In addition, ΔNE was significantly associated with repeated WST-1 reduction ($F(1/34) = 0.29$, $p = .597$, $\eta_p{}^2 = .01$) while controlling for group, which lost its prior significance ($p = .60$). Neither EPI nor cortisol change coefficients were found to mediate repeated macrophage microbicidal potential, as both measures did not relate to repeated WST-1 reduction after controlling for group ($p's > .64$). Post-hoc correlation analyses showed that higher ΔNE levels were associated with lower WST-1 reduction scores immediately ($r = -.49$, $p = .01$), 10 ($r = -.33$, $p = .07$), and 60 min ($r = -.55$, $p = .001$) after TSST / rest.

Table 3.

Partial correlations between WST-1 reduction measures and stress hormone change coefficients after controlling for age, MAP, and BMI.

Stress hormone change	WST-1 reduction time points after TSST / rest		
	+0 min	+10 min	+60 min
ΔNE (pg/ml)	-.49*	-.33	-.55*
ΔEPI (pg/ml)	-.22	-.32	-.05
ΔCORT (nmol/l)	-.22	-.30	-.26

Notes. Stress hormone changes (ΔNE, ΔEPI, ΔCORT) refer to the difference between the expected stress peak level minus baseline. NE, norepinephrine; EPI, epinephrine; CORT, cortisol; MAP, mean arterial blood pressure; BMI, body mass index; $*p < .01$.

3.2.4 Discussion

To our knowledge, this is the first study to test whether macrophage microbicidal potential is reduced by acute psychological stress and whether this stress effect is statistically mediated by treatment (stress vs. rest)-induced stress hormone change. We used the WST-1 macrophage assay based on the reduction of WST-1 by O_2^- produced by PMA-activated *ex vivo* isolated HMDM (Kuebler et al., submitted), and measured plasma levels of the stress hormones NE, EPI, and cortisol.

As hypothesized, we found a stress-induced decrease in WST-1 reduction of PMA-activated *ex vivo* isolated HMDM. WST-1 reduction by HMDM of the stressed subjects remained unchanged throughout the study period, whereas HMDM of the controls showed an increase in WST-1 reduction over time. This stress-induced decrease in macrophage microbicidal potential was statistically mediated by NE changes but did not significantly relate to EPI and cortisol changes. Higher NE stress responses (ΔNE) were associated with lower scores of WST-1 reduction by HMDM. Our findings suggest that the microbicidal potential of HMDM is reduced by acute psychological stress, and that this stress effect is mediated by treatment (stress vs. rest)-induced changes in NE plasma levels.

What are the potential implications of these findings and how do they relate to the literature? In contrast to our stressed subjects, we found that microbicidal macrophage potential of the controls increased in terms of WST-1 reduction over time. We intentionally aimed for this finding as we applied a standardized wound by simple insertion of a venous catheter more than two hours (165 min) prior to stress induction. After a review of the wound healing literature, we thought this time interval to be sufficiently long to allow initiation of wound healing processes and thus monocyte priming stimulation (Mahdavian Delavary et al., 2011; Stroncek & Reichert, 2008). Consequently, we interpret the observed continuous increase in microbicidal macrophage potential as reflecting successful wound healing initiation. Thus, our open wound paradigm seems to work in the expected direction.

Our main finding is that microbicidal potential of HMDM of the stressed subjects remained unchanged throughout the study period. Psychological stress has been repeatedly shown to delay the process of wound healing (Gouin & Kiecolt-Glaser, 2011; Walburn et al., 2009) in which macrophages are known to play a pivotal role (Mahdavian Delavary et al., 2011). Skin wound healing characteristically runs in consecutive and overlapping phases with the inflammatory phase as an early phase beginning within hours after wound administration (Stroncek & Reichert, 2008). This phase aims at eliminating potential microbes, foreign particles and cell debris in the wound (Mahdavian Delavary et al., 2011;

Stroncek & Reichert, 2008). After approximately 48 hours, the most prominent immune cells in the wound area are monocyte-derived macrophages, probably of the M1 macrophage phenotype (Engelhardt et al., 1998; Mahdavian Delavary et al., 2011; Stroncek & Reichert, 2008). These M1 macrophages are essential for successful completion of the inflammatory phase: They kill microbes by microbicidal activity and also promote inflammation by secreting pro-inflammatory cytokines, thus contributing to the progression to the next levels of wound healing (Martinez et al., 2008; Taylor et al., 2005). Notably, the stimulation method used in our study is known to result in M1 macrophages, i.e. our HMDM represent M1 macrophages (Martinez et al., 2008). After successful cleaning of the wound, macrophages appear to change their functional phenotype into M2 macrophages, which show increased effector functions important for the next phases of wound healing (Stout & Suttles, 2004). Given the importance of our HMDM as tissue M1 macrophages (Duffield, 2003; Gordon, 2003; Mahdavian Delavary et al., 2011; Porcheray et al., 2005), our findings suggest that the stress-induced delay in wound healing may be mediated by suppression of M1 macrophage microbicidal potential, the necessary precondition for microbicidal activity. Moreover, our cross-sectional analyses suggest that the stress-induced release of NE seems to mediate the stress-induced attenuation of microbicidal macrophage potential.

What mechanisms may underlie the observed findings? We propose the following hypothesized process to explain the NE-mediated wound healing attenuation in the stress group as compared to the resting control group: NE inhibits LPS-induced production of pro-inflammatory cytokines such as TNF-α (van der Poll et al., 1994; Verhoeckx et al., 2005). Given this ability of NE to inhibit stimulated cytokine release by monocytes, NE may inhibit monocytes / macrophage cytokine release (1) either during the *in vivo* wound-priming period when wound application-induced thrombin release may stimulate cytokine release and / or (2) during the *in vitro* differentiation period when LPS, TNF-α, and IFN-γ are used as stimulating agents. Consequently, NE may reduce cytokine concentrations and thus lower expression of NADPH oxidase subunits as prerequisites of PMA-induced NADPH oxidase activation. Figure 13 depicts the proposed process in detail.

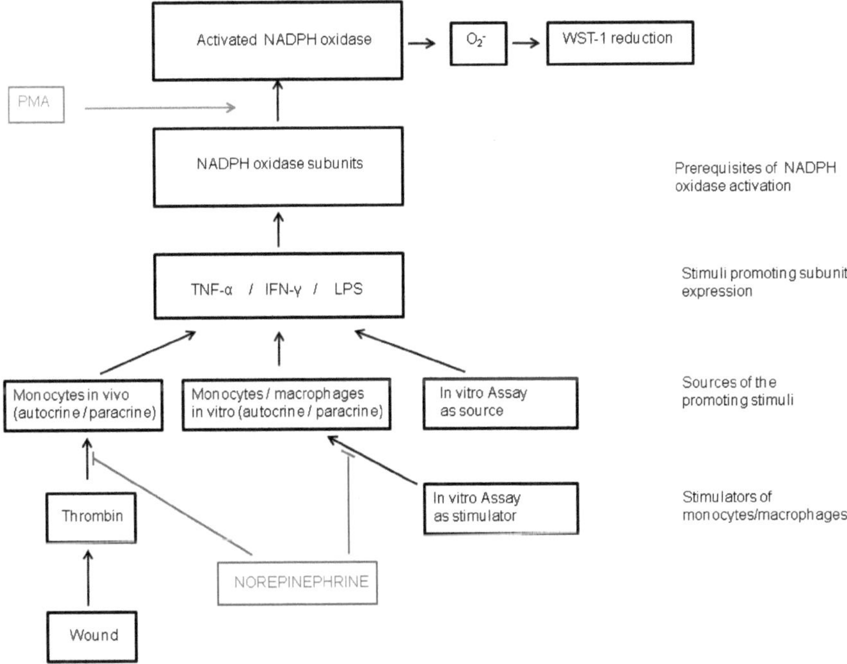

Figure 13. Proposed process to explain stress-induced wound healing attenuation.

Mechanism of superoxide anion production and subsequent WST-1 reduction. An increase in O_2^- induced WST-1 reduction results from the activation of the enzyme complex NADPH oxidase (Sakai et al., 2009). Activation of NADPH oxidase is induced by phosphorylation of cytosolic subunits (hitherto identified subunits: p67phox, p47phox, p40phox, and RacGDP) and their subsequent translocation to membrane-bound subunits (hitherto identified: gp91phox p22phox) to form the complex (El-Benna et al., 2005). Notably, higher activation by a higher amount of NADPH oxidase complex formation results in higher O_2^- reduction (Sakai et al., 2009). An increase in NADPH oxidase complex formation is likely to result from increases in the number of NADPH oxidase subunits combined with phosphorylation of cytosolic subunits (Sakai et al., 2009). Our *in vitro* assay comprises cytokine and LPS-induced stimulation of the expression of the NADPH oxidase subunits p22phox, p47phox, and p67phox, and subsequent activation with PMA, a substance that activates PKC, which in turn induces phosphorylation of cytosolic subunits (Bedard & Krause, 2007; Sakai et al., 2009). Thus, our 48h incubation procedure induces superoxide anion production in a standardized way.

Our control group showed an increase in O_2^- induced WST-1 reduction over time. Given that the four samples of a control person (obtained during an 80-min interval starting 165 min after catheter insertion) showed an increasing O_2^- production over time, and given the standardized *in vitro* stimulation procedure, we assume that the catheter insertion (and thus the open wound application) may promote additional expression of NADPH oxidase subunits prior to the standardized *in vitro* stimulation procedure. Indeed, wound induction promotes thrombocytes to secrete the enzyme thrombin (He et al., 2010). Thrombin in turn stimulates monocytes to secrete inflammatory cytokines such as IFN-γ and TNF-α, which may further stimulate monocytes by autocrine and paracrine signal mediation (Mahdavian Delavary et al., 2011). Interestingly, IFN-γ and TNF-α are both capable of stimulating expression of NADPH oxidase subunits (Gauss et al., 2007; Schroder et al., 2004). IFN-γ also increases expression of TLR 4, a well-known LPS-receptor (Schroder et al., 2004). LPS (which is used as a stimulant in the subsequent standardized stimulation procedure) similarly increases NADPH oxidase subunit expression (DeLeo et al., 1998). In sum, this prior activation is assumed to result in increased NADPH oxidase subunit and LPS-receptor expression and may thus represent a kind of wound-induced priming of circulating monocytes as the precursors of M1 macrophages. We speculate that this hypothesized priming effect is responsible for the increase in O_2^- production over time in our control group.

We observed lower WST-1 reduction in our stress group that is statistically mediated by NE increases. NE has been repeatedly shown to inhibit LPS-induced production of pro-inflammatory cytokines such as TNF-α (van der Poll et al., 1994; Verhoeckx et al., 2005). Given the NE-induced inhibition of stimulated cytokine release by monocytes, NE may inhibit monocyte / macrophage cytokine release either during the *in vivo* wound priming period and / or during the *in vitro* differentiation period when LPS, TNF-α, and IFN-γ are used as stimulating agents. Consequently, NE may reduce cytokine concentrations and thus lower expression of NADPH oxidase subunits as prerequisites of NADPH oxidase activation.

Some limitations of our study must be reported. First, we activated NADPH oxidase supraphysiologically using the synthetic stimulus PMA leading to increased NADPH oxidase activity in comparison to natural stimuli (Sakai et al., 2009; Siddiqi et al., 2001). We can only speculate as to whether stress reduces physiologically activated NADPH oxidase activity. Second, our methodological approach does not allow exact macrophage numbers to be counted as macrophages became adherent in a multilayered way in cell culture plates (Kuebler et al., submitted). Notably, this maximum number of adherent macrophages is necessary to guarantee a sufficient electron release able to reliably induce measurable WST-1 reduction (Sakai et al., 2009). However, we standardized numbers of isolated PBMC to guarantee excess amounts of monocytes as precursor cells. Indeed, stress-induced suppression of macrophage microbicidal potential could be observed not only immediately after stress when leukocyte subset redistribution occurs, but also 10 min and as a trend 60 min after stress cessation when leukocyte redistribution is known to be over (Buske-Kirschbaum, Kern, Ebrecht, & Hellhammer, 2007). Thus, subtle differences in monocyte ratios within the isolated PBMC fractions seem negligible for WST-1 reduction. It might be speculated that the area of the cell culture plate may restrict adherence of developing macrophages. Third, our mediation analysis is of a statistical nature. Although cross-sectional results clearly indicate mediation by NE, experimental studies are needed to verify this finding. Fourth, our findings are restricted to healthy, medication-free, non-smoking men. Further studies are needed to replicate our findings in other samples and settings.

Our study does also have various strengths: It is the first human study to investigate macrophage potential after wound application. It combines both *in vivo* wound application and stress induction and *in vitro* measurement of M1 microbicidal potential. In addition to the fact that our study design included a resting control group, a further strength was the standardized and simple wound application paradigm initiating wound healing processes in a natural manner. Furthermore, as monocytes / macrophages represent the dominating leukocyte subpopulation in the wound area for approximately 48 hours after wound administration (Engelhardt et al., 1998; Mahdavian Delavary et al., 2011; Stroncek & Reichert, 2008), our 48h-PBMC *in vitro* incubation period was intended to create maximum numbers of monocyte-derived M1 macrophages that possibly resemble *in vivo* macrophage activation processes at wound sites.

In sum, our findings suggest that microbicidal potential as the precondition for microbicidal activity of human M1 macrophages seems to be inhibited by acute psychological stress. Furthermore, the mechanism by which stress decreases HMDM' microbicidal potential may involve NE stress responses. Our findings might have implications for wound healing.

4 Discussion

Having presented and discussed in detail in the previous chapter the results of the studies that underlie the present thesis, in this chapter the results from both studies will be considered on a general level. The major findings are first summarized briefly. The theoretical implications of the findings are then discussed and positioned within the current research context. This is followed by a reflection on the research approach before considering possibilities for future research and drawing a conclusion in the final section.

4.1 Summary of the results

4.1.1 A simple in vitro method to investigate the microbicidal potential of human macrophages

The aim of this study, and at the same time a condition for the second study, was to implement and validate a simple and cost-efficient *in vitro* method for assessing microbicidal potential of HMDM.

The method used in this study is a colorimetric *in vitro* assay which was previously applied successfully in cells of the THP-1 cell line (Sakai et al., 2009). During a 48-hour incubation step the monocytes isolated from blood are differentiated to HMDM with the addition of LPS, IFN-γ and TNF-α. The production of O_2^- and the microbicidal potential of the HMDM were activated by PMA. The assay used the salt WST-1, which changes color to yellow in the presence of O_2^-, to measure the O_2^- production. This method was implemented and validated in 21 healthy male subjects. For the validation we used a reference method which activated the production of O_2^- in macrophages in a similar manner to the *in vitro* assay that was used (Sakai et al., 2009).

In the HMDM of all the subjects O_2^- production could be activated and measured. Furthermore, these results correlated well with those of the reference method. Overall, our results confirm the successful use of a simple and cost-efficient *in vitro* method to assess the NADPH oxidase-mediated microbicidal potential of HMDM.

4.1.2 Acute stress reduces the microbicidal potential of *ex vivo* isolated human monocyte-derived macrophages

This study planned to investigate the effects of an acute psychological stressor on the microbicidal potential of HMDM within a wound paradigm. A further goal was to verify whether potential stress effects are mediated via the stress hormones NE, EPI and / or cortisol.

A total of 41 healthy male subjects were studied. Acute psychological stress was induced in half of the sample. To allow initiation of wound healing processes, a standardized wound was inflicted by insertion of a venous catheter more than two hours prior to stress induction. The microbicidal potential and the O_2^- production of the HMDM were elevated before and during one hour after stress / rest. Furthermore, plasma NE and EPI levels as well as salivary cortisol were repeatedly measured.

We found a stress-induced decrease in O_2^- production of HMDM. O_2^- production by HMDM in the stressed subjects remained unchanged throughout the study period whereas HMDM in the controls showed an increase in O_2^- production over time. This stress-induced decrease in macrophage microbicidal potential was statistically mediated by NE changes. Thus, our results suggest that acute psychological stress reduces NADPH oxidase-mediated microbicidal potential of HMDM probably via NE release.

4.2 Discussion of the results

Both human and animal studies have repeatedly yielded empirical evidence that acute as well as chronic psychological stress delays skin wound healing (Gouin & Kiecolt-Glaser, 2011; Walburn et al., 2009). The precise mechanisms by which psychological stress impairs wound healing are, however, still largely unknown (Gouin & Kiecolt-Glaser, 2011). The primary aim of this thesis was therefore to make some progress towards clarifying the mechanism that mediates these stress effects.

The suppressive effect of acute psychological stress on the microbicidal potential of HMDM after wound infliction, which also appears to be mediated by NE, that was revealed in this study actually points to a possible mechanism by which psychological stress, at least in part, delays wound healing in the skin. This hypothesis is implicitly supported by current research findings.

Findings from various fields of research suggest that psychological stress mediated via the HPA axis and the SNS or via glucocorticoids and the CA EPI and NE suppresses the immune system in the wound area during the inflammatory phase of wound healing. For example, an animal study carried out by Rojas and colleagues assumed that psychological stress during the inflammatory phase attenuated the microbicidal activity in the wound area with a subsequent delay in wound healing (Rojas et al., 2002). The microbicidal activity in the study by Rojas and colleagues was operationalized using the extent of bacterial colonization in the wound area, which was significantly elevated under stress.

According to the literature microbes are eliminated from the wound area during the inflammatory phase shortly after injury primarily by inflammatory M1 macrophages - specifically, by the macrophage phenotype that forms the subject of this thesis (Engelhardt et al., 1998; Mahdavian Delavary et al., 2011; Stroncek & Reichert, 2008).

Furthermore, it has been repeatedly demonstrated that the stress effects that hinder the progress of wound healing are associated with a lowered pro-inflammatory cytokine concentration in the wound area (Christian, Graham, Padgett, Glaser, & Kiecolt-Glaser, 2006; Godbout & Glaser, 2006; Gouin & Kiecolt-Glaser, 2011). At first glance these findings do not appear to support our hypothesis that psychological stress exerts its negative effects on the progress of wound healing partly via the reduction in microbicidal potential and thus in microbicidal activity of human macrophages. However, in light of the fact that ROS not only act as microbicidal agents but also as ligands which can boost the pro-inflammatory cytokine release in an autocrine and paracrine manner by manipulating the activity of transcription factors (for details see section 2.1.2.6), these findings can also be interpreted as being consistent with the results of our study.

Especially findings from animal studies suggest that the delay in wound healing, and very likely the immune suppressing effects of stress as well, are mediated by GC, NE and EPI (Denda et al., 2000; Kao et al., 2003; Padgett et al., 1998; Pullar, Grahn et al., 2006; Pullar, Rizzo et al., 2006; Rojas et al., 2002; Sivamani et al., 2009). Because monocytes / macrophages are known to express receptors for a range of different neuroendocrine products of the HPA axis and the SNS (Blotta et al., 1997; Reyes-Garcia and Garcia-Tamayo, 2009; Rouppe van der Voort et al., 2000; Woods, 2000), meaning they are susceptible to the influence of psychological stress in general, our findings can also be considered consistent with the available evidence in the context of wound healing.

Our findings also indicated that the stress hormone NE mediates the suppressive effects of psychological stress on the microbicidal potential of M1 macrophages following wound infliction. This finding can also be easily integrated into the current research context. NE is considered a hormone that generally inhibits M1 macrophage activity (Reyes-Garcia & Garcia-Tamayo, 2009). While until recently the role of GC was still considered primarily responsible for stress-induced delays in the progress of wound healing (Godbout & Glaser, 2006), the latest findings from animal studies have corroborated the hypothesis that the stress hormones NE and EPI also mediate the negative effects of psychological stress on wound healing in addition to GC (Pullar, Grahn et al., 2006; Pullar, Rizzo et al., 2006; Sivamani et al., 2009).

As outlined in section 2.3.1.2, the effects of GC on monocytes / macrophages are dependent on various factors, including the activation status of the cells (Stanojevic et al., 2007). In the activated state monocytes / macrophages appear to be less sensitive to GC effects - possibly as a result of reduced expression of GC receptors (Stanojevic et al., 2007). As a result of the infliction of a wound (catheter insertion) more than 2 hours prior to the induction of psychological stress, there has most likely been *in vivo* stimulation of the monocytes in the blood (Mahdavian Delavary et al., 2011), which is also supported by the detectable increase in the microbicidal potential of M1 macrophages over time in the control group. This *in vivo* stimulation could be the reason for the absence of GC effects on the microbicidal potential of the HMDM in our study.

Taken together, our results are consistent with the existing literature and support the assertion that acute psychological stress mediates parts of its negative effects on the progress of wound healing by reducing microbicidal potential and thus the microbicidal activity of M1 macrophages.

4.3 Methodological reflection

Our study design is characterized by various strengths. The wound paradigm, i.e. the infliction of an open wound by inserting a catheter, enabled the wound healing process to be initiated and thus the effect of acute psychological stress on an already stimulated or primed immune system to be studied analogous to other wound healing studies (Stroncek & Reichert, 2008). The integration of a control group, which was not exposed to a psychological stressor, enabled the stress effect to be determined using a direct comparison between the stress and control groups. The implemented assay we used also enabled samples to be processed immediately after blood was taken, thus ensuring optimal conditions for the isolated cells. Due to the 48-hour incubation time and the differentiation stimuli (LPS, IFN-γ, TNF-α), this assay enabled us to study an M1 macrophage *in vitro* that resembles a macrophage phenotype *in vivo* at a point in time when this is likely to be the dominant immune cell subtype in the wound area (Engelhardt et al., 1998; Mahdavian Delavary et al., 2011; Martinez et al., 2008; Stroncek & Reichert, 2008).

Likewise there are some limitations to the study design. Our wound paradigm does not yield any information about the consequences of a reduction in the microbicidal potential of M1 macrophages that is induced by psychological stress for the subsequent progress of wound healing. Moreover, the *in vitro* environment is not remotely as complex as the *in vivo* environment, meaning that the effects of psychological stress on the microbicidal potential of M1 macrophages which we could observe *in vitro* may not be found in this form *in vivo* - although our findings can be easily integrated with current research findings which supports the generalization from *in vitro* to *in vivo*. Limitations also apply to the NE effect. According to our data the stress hormone NE mediates the effects of psychological stress on macrophages. This finding is based on cross-sectional data which do not yield any information about causal relationships. Furthermore, the data were assessed in healthy male subjects. It is impossible to generalize the finding to other subpopulations. An additional, but final, criticism refers to our implemented *in vitro* assay: we did not determine the assay quality indicators, assay sensitivity and stability. However, our data indicate that these indices should be in an appropriate range.

4.4   Conclusion and directions for future studies

To the best of our knowledge, this is the first research project to investigate the effect of acute psychological stress on microbicidal potential of HMDM within a wound paradigm. In conclusion, our findings suggest that acute psychological stress exerts the retarding effects on wound healing at least in part by reducing the microbicidal potential of macrophages that are newly recruited from the blood and classically activated in the wound area, and that, in turn, these immunosuppressive stress effects are possibly mediated by NE, an assumption which is also supported by current research results.

One of the first steps in future research should be the replication of these results in different subpopulations such as women or a different age cohort. In this regard, an extension of such a study design could refer to the assessment of the pro-inflammatory cytokine release by M1 macrophages as a dependent variable in addition to the microbicidal potential.

Future research should also explore the existing data set in terms of associations between other psychological states as well as traits and stress reactivity of macrophages' microbicidal potential.

Especially in human studies, health behavior such as smoking or leisure-time physical activity should be taken into account when exploring the relationship between psychological stress, the immune system and health outcomes. Consequently, studies are needed to investigate the effect of psychological stress on microbicidal potential of macrophages within our wound paradigm in smokers or amateur athletes, for instance.

Finally, the implication of NE as a mediator of the link between psychological stress and microbicidal potential of macrophages after wounding should be further studied – possibly by testing NE infusion effects on macrophages' microbicidal potential.

Stress-delayed wound healing is associated with slower and more complicated postoperative recovery (Kiecolt-Glaser et al., 1998). A better understanding of the mechanisms of how psychological stress delays wound healing may provide important information for developing strategies of interdisciplinary intervention programs with the goal of improving the healing process. The results presented in this thesis might encourage ongoing research in this field of PNI.

5 References

Abbas, A., Lichtman, A., Pillai, S. (2007). *Cellular and molecular immunology.* Elsevier: China.

Adams, D. O. (1994). Molecular biology of macrophage activation: a pathway whereby psychosocial factors can potentially affect health. *Psychosom Med, 56*(4), 316-327.

Adams, D. O., & Hamilton, T. A. (1984). The cell biology of macrophage activation. *Annu Rev Immunol, 2,* 283-318.

Almeida, A. C., Rehder, J., Severino, S. D., Martins-Filho, J., Newburger, P. E., & Condino-Neto, A. (2005). The effect of IFN-gamma and TNF-alpha on the NADPH oxidase system of human colostrum macrophages, blood monocytes, and THP-1 cells. *J Interferon Cytokine Res, 25*(9), 540-546.

Altemus, M., Rao, B., Dhabhar, F. S., Ding, W., & Granstein, R. D. (2001). Stress-induced changes in skin barrier function in healthy women. *J Invest Dermatol, 117*(2), 309-317.

Alvarez, B., & Radi, R. (2003). Peroxynitrite reactivity with amino acids and proteins. *Amino Acids, 25*(3-4), 295-311.

Atanackovic, D., Schulze, J., Kroger, H., Brunner-Weinzierl, M. C., & Deter, H. C. (2003). Acute psychological stress induces a prolonged suppression of the production of reactive oxygen species by phagocytes. *J Neuroimmunol, 142*(1-2), 159-165.

Auffray, C., Sieweke, M. H., & Geissmann, F. (2009). Blood monocytes: development, heterogeneity, and relationship with dendritic cells. *Annu Rev Immunol, 27,* 669-692.

Auphan, N., DiDonato, J. A., Rosette, C., Helmberg, A., & Karin, M. (1995). Immunosuppression by glucocorticoids: inhibition of NF-kappa B activity through induction of I kappa B synthesis. *Science, 270*(5234), 286-290.

Auwerx, J. (1991). The human leukemia cell line, THP-1: a multifacetted model for the study of monocyte-macrophage differentiation. *Experientia, 47*(1), 22-31.

Babior, B. M. (1984). Oxidants from phagocytes: agents of defense and destruction. *Blood, 64*(5), 959-966.

Babior, B. M. (2000). Phagocytes and oxidative stress. *Am J Med, 109*(1), 33-44.

Babior, B. M., Lambeth, J. D., & Nauseef, W. (2002). The neutrophil NADPH oxidase. *Arch Biochem Biophys, 397*(2), 342-344.

Barish, G. D., Downes, M., Alaynick, W. A., Yu, R. T., Ocampo, C. B., Bookout, A. L., et al. (2005). A Nuclear Receptor Atlas: macrophage activation. *Mol Endocrinol, 19*(10), 2466-2477.

Barnes, P. J. (2010). Mechanisms and resistance in glucocorticoid control of inflammation. *J Steroid Biochem Mol Biol, 120*(2-3), 76-85.

Baum, C. L., & Arpey, C. J. (2005). Normal cutaneous wound healing: clinical correlation with cellular and molecular events. *Dermatol Surg, 31*(6), 674-686; discussion 686.

Beato, M., Herrlich, P., & Schutz, G. (1995). Steroid hormone receptors: many actors in search of a plot. *Cell, 83*(6), 851-857.

Beck, G., Brinkkoetter, P., Hanusch, C., Schulte, J., van Ackern, K., van der Woude, F. J., et al. (2004). Clinical review: immunomodulatory effects of dopamine in general inflammation. *Crit Care, 8*(6), 485-491.

Bedard, K., & Krause, K. H. (2007). The NOX family of ROS-generating NADPH oxidases: physiology and pathophysiology. *Physiol Rev, 87*(1), 245-313.

Birbaumer, N., & Schmidt, R. F. (2010). *Biologische Psycholgie.* Heidelberg: Springer.

Blotta, M. H., DeKruyff, R. H., & Umetsu, D. T. (1997). Corticosteroids inhibit IL-12 production in human monocytes and enhance their capacity to induce IL-4 synthesis in CD4+ lymphocytes. *J Immunol, 158*(12), 5589-5595.

Bokoch, G. M. (1995). Chemoattractant signaling and leukocyte activation. *Blood, 86*(5), 1649-1660.

Bokoch, G. M., & Diebold, B. A. (2002). Current molecular models for NADPH oxidase regulation by Rac GTPase. *Blood, 100*(8), 2692-2696.

Bosco, M. C., Musso, T., Carta, L., & Vaersio, L. (2000). Analysis of macrophage lytic functions. In D. M. Paulnock (Ed), *Macrophages* (pp. 127-155), Athens: Oxford Universtiy Press.

Brandes, R. P., & Janiszewski, M. (2005). Direct detection of reactive oxygen species ex vivo. *Kidney Int, 67*(5), 1662-1664.

Breitkreutz, D., Mirancea, N., & Nischt, R. (2009). Basement membranes in skin: unique matrix structures with diverse functions? *Histochem Cell Biol, 132*(1), 1-10.

Buckley, T. M., & Schatzberg, A. F. (2005). On the interactions of the hypothalamic-pituitary-adrenal (HPA) axis and sleep: normal HPA axis activity and circadian rhythm, exemplary sleep disorders. *J Clin Endocrinol Metab, 90*(5), 3106-3114.

Buske-Kirschbaum, A., Kern, S., Ebrecht, M., & Hellhammer, D. H. (2007). Altered distribution of leukocyte subsets and cytokine production in response to acute psychosocial stress in patients with psoriasis vulgaris. *Brain Behav Immun, 21*(1), 92-99.

Buttgereit, F., & Scheffold, A. (2002). Rapid glucocorticoid effects on immune cells. *Steroids, 67*(6), 529-534.

Cannon, W. B. (1915). *Bodily changes in pain, hunger, fear and rage: An account of recent researchers into the function of emotional excitement.* New York: Appelton.

Cannon, W. B. (1939). *The wisdom of the body.* New York: W. W. Norton.

Cathcart, M. K. (2004). Regulation of superoxide anion production by NADPH oxidase in monocytes/macrophages: contributions to atherosclerosis. *Arterioscler Thromb Vasc Biol, 24*(1), 23-28.

Cepika, A. M., Bendelja, K., Vergles, J. M., Malenica, B., Kapitanovic, S., & Gagro, A. (2010). Monocyte response to LPS after exposure to corticosteroids and chloroquine with implications for systemic lupus erythematosus. *Scand J Immunol, 72*(5), 434-443.

Chizzolini, C., Rezzonico, R., De Luca, C., Burger, D., & Dayer, J. M. (2000). Th2 cell membrane factors in association with IL-4 enhance matrix metalloproteinase-1 (MMP-1) while decreasing MMP-9 production by granulocyte-macrophage colony-stimulating factor-differentiated human monocytes. *J Immunol, 164*(11), 5952-5960.

Christian, L. M., Graham, J. E., Padgett, D. A., Glaser, R., & Kiecolt-Glaser, J. K. (2006). Stress and wound healing. *Neuroimmunomodulation, 13*(5-6), 337-346.

Cohen, J., Ward, G., Prins, J., Jones, M., & Venkatesh, B. (2006). Variability of cortisol assays can confound the diagnosis of adrenal insufficiency in the critically ill population. *Intensive Care Med, 32*(11), 1901-1905.

A controlled trial of interferon gamma to prevent infection in chronic granulomatous disease. The International Chronic Granulomatous Disease Cooperative Study Group. (1991). *N Engl J Med, 324*(8), 509-516.

Couto, M. A., Liu, L., Lehrer, R. I., & Ganz, T. (1994). Inhibition of intracellular Histoplasma capsulatum replication by murine macrophages that produce human defensin. *Infect Immun, 62*(6), 2375-2378.

Croxtall, J. D., Choudhury, Q., & Flower, R. J. (2000). Glucocorticoids act within minutes to inhibit recruitment of signalling factors to activated EGF receptors through a receptor-dependent, transcription-independent mechanism. *Br J Pharmacol, 130*(2), 289-298.

Daems, W. T., & de Bakker, J. M. (1982). Do resident macrophages proliferate? *Immunobiology, 161*(3-4), 204-211.

Dale, D. C., Boxer, L., & Liles, W. C. (2008). The phagocytes: neutrophils and monocytes. *Blood, 112*(4), 935-945.

Daley, J. M., Brancato, S. K., Thomay, A. A., Reichner, J. S., & Albina, J. E. (2010). The phenotype of murine wound macrophages. *J Leukoc Biol, 87*(1), 59-67.

Dalton, D. K., Pitts-Meek, S., Keshav, S., Figari, I. S., Bradley, A., & Stewart, T. A. (1993). Multiple defects of immune cell function in mice with disrupted interferon-gamma genes. *Science, 259*(5102), 1739-1742.

Dalton, T. P., Shertzer, H. G., & Puga, A. (1999). Regulation of gene expression by reactive oxygen. *Annu Rev Pharmacol Toxicol, 39*, 67-101.

DeLeo, F. R., Renee, J., McCormick, S., Nakamura, M., Apicella, M., Weiss, J. P., et al. (1998). Neutrophils exposed to bacterial lipopolysaccharide upregulate NADPH oxidase assembly. *J Clin Invest, 101*(2), 455-463.

Denda, M., Tsuchiya, T., Elias, P. M., & Feingold, K. R. (2000). Stress alters cutaneous permeability barrier homeostasis. *Am J Physiol Regul Integr Comp Physiol, 278*(2), R367-372.

DeRijk, R. H., Schaaf, M., & de Kloet, E. R. (2002). Glucocorticoid receptor variants: clinical implications. *J Steroid Biochem Mol Biol, 81*(2), 103-122.

Devalaraja, R. M., Nanney, L. B., Du, J., Qian, Q., Yu, Y., Devalaraja, M. N., et al. (2000). Delayed wound healing in CXCR2 knockout mice. *J Invest Dermatol, 115*(2), 234-244.

Dickerson, S. S., & Kemeny, M. E. (2004). Acute stressors and cortisol responses: a theoretical integration and synthesis of laboratory research. *Psychol Bull, 130*(3), 355-391.

Dragos, D., & Tanasescu, M. D. (2010). The effect of stress on the defense systems. *J Med Life, 3*(1), 10-18.

Duffield, J. S. (2003). The inflammatory macrophage: a story of Jekyll and Hyde. *Clin Sci (Lond), 104*(1), 27-38.

Dunston, C. R., & Griffiths, H. R. (2010). The effect of ageing on macrophage Toll-like receptor-mediated responses in the fight against pathogens. *Clin Exp Immunol, 161*(3), 407-416.

Edwards, S., Clow, A., Evans, P., & Hucklebridge, F. (2001). Exploration of the awakening cortisol response in relation to diurnal cortisol secretory activity. *Life Sci, 68*(18), 2093-2103.

Ehlert, U., Gaab, J., & Heinrichs, M. (2001). Psychoneuroendocrinological contributions to the etiology of depression, posttraumatic stress disorder, and stress-related bodily disorders: the role of the hypothalamus-pituitary-adrenal axis. *Biol Psychol, 57*(1-3), 141-152.

Ehlert, U., & von Känel (2010). *Psychoendokrinologie und Psychonimmunologie.* Springer: Berlin.

Ehlert, U. (2010). Das endokrine System. In U. Ehlert, & R. von Känel (Eds), *Psychoendokrinologie und Psychoimmunologie* (pp. 3-37). Springer: Berlin.

Ehrchen, J., Steinmuller, L., Barczyk, K., Tenbrock, K., Nacken, W., Eisenacher, M., et al. (2007). Glucocorticoids induce differentiation of a specifically activated, anti-inflammatory subtype of human monocytes. *Blood, 109*(3), 1265-1274.

Ehrenreich, H., Schuck, J., Stender, N., Pilz, J., Gefeller, O., Schilling, L., et al. (1997). Endocrine and hemodynamic effects of stress versus systemic CRF in alcoholics during early and medium term abstinence. *Alcohol Clin Exp Res, 21*(7), 1285-1293.

Eierman, D. F., Johnson, C. E., & Haskill, J. S. (1989). Human monocyte inflammatory mediator gene expression is selectively regulated by adherence substrates. *J Immunol, 142*(6), 1970-1976.

El-Benna, J., Dang, P. M., Gougerot-Pocidalo, M. A., & Elbim, C. (2005). Phagocyte NADPH oxidase: a multicomponent enzyme essential for host defenses. *Arch Immunol Ther Exp (Warsz), 53*(3), 199-206.

Elenkov, I. J., Wilder, R. L., Chrousos, G. P., & Vizi, E. S. (2000). The sympathetic nerve--an integrative interface between two supersystems: the brain and the immune system. *Pharmacol Rev, 52*(4), 595-638.

Ellard, D. R., Castle, P. C., & Mian, R. (2001). The effect of a short-term mental stressor on neutrophil activation. *Int J Psychophysiol, 41*(1), 93-100.

Elsdale, T., & Bard, J. (1972). Collagen substrata for studies on cell behavior. *J Cell Biol,* *54*(3), 626-637.

Eming, S. A., Krieg, T., & Davidson, J. M. (2007). Inflammation in wound repair: molecular and cellular mechanisms. *J Invest Dermatol, 127*(3), 514-525.

Eming, S. A., Smola, H., & Krieg, T. (2002). Treatment of chronic wounds: state of the art and future concepts. *Cells Tissues Organs, 172*(2), 105-117.

Engelhardt, E., Toksoy, A., Goebeler, M., Debus, S., Brocker, E. B., & Gillitzer, R. (1998). Chemokines IL-8, GROalpha, MCP-1, IP-10, and Mig are sequentially and differentially expressed during phase-specific infiltration of leukocyte subsets in human wound healing. *Am J Pathol, 153*(6), 1849-1860.

Engler, D., Pham, T., Fullerton, M. J., Ooi, G., Funder, J. W., & Clarke, I. J. (1989). Studies of the secretion of corticotropin-releasing factor and arginine vasopressin into the hypophysial-portal circulation of the conscious sheep. I. Effect of an audiovisual stimulus and insulin-induced hypoglycemia. *Neuroendocrinology, 49*(4), 367-381.

Fadok, V. A., Bratton, D. L., Konowal, A., Freed, P. W., Westcott, J. Y., & Henson, P. M. (1998). Macrophages that have ingested apoptotic cells in vitro inhibit proinflammatory cytokine production through autocrine/paracrine mechanisms involving TGF-beta, PGE2, and PAF. *J Clin Invest, 101*(4), 890-898.

Fang, F. C. (2004). Antimicrobial reactive oxygen and nitrogen species: concepts and controversies. *Nat Rev Microbiol, 2*(10), 820-832.

Finkel, T. (2003). Oxidant signals and oxidative stress. *Curr Opin Cell Biol, 15*(2), 247-254.

Folkman, S. (1997). Positive psychological states and coping with severe stress. *Soc Sci Med, 45*(8), 1207-1221.

Forman, H. J., & Torres, M. (2002). Reactive oxygen species and cell signaling: respiratory burst in macrophage signaling. *Am J Respir Crit Care Med, 166*(12 Pt 2), S4-8.

Fridovich, I. (1997). Superoxide anion radical (O2-.), superoxide dismutases, and related matters. *J Biol Chem, 272*(30), 18515-18517.

Gailit, J., & Clark, R. A. (1994). Wound repair in the context of extracellular matrix. *Curr Opin Cell Biol, 6*(5), 717-725.

Garcia, J. J., del Carmen Saez, M., De la Fuente, M., & Ortega, E. (2003). Regulation of phagocytic process of macrophages by noradrenaline and its end metabolite 4-hydroxy-3-metoxyphenyl-glycol. Role of alpha- and beta-adrenoreceptors. *Mol Cell Biochem, 254*(1-2), 299-304.

Gathercole, L. L., & Stewart, P. M. (2010). Targeting the pre-receptor metabolism of cortisol as a novel therapy in obesity and diabetes. *J Steroid Biochem Mol Biol, 122*(1-3), 21-27.

Gauss, K. A., Nelson-Overton, L. K., Siemsen, D. W., Gao, Y., DeLeo, F. R., & Quinn, M. T. (2007). Role of NF-kappaB in transcriptional regulation of the phagocyte NADPH oxidase by tumor necrosis factor-alpha. *J Leukoc Biol, 82*(3), 729-741.

Geissmann, F., Jung, S., & Littman, D. R. (2003). Blood monocytes consist of two principal subsets with distinct migratory properties. *Immunity, 19*(1), 71-82.

George, A. A., Schiltz, R. L., & Hager, G. L. (2009). Dynamic access of the glucocorticoid receptor to response elements in chromatin. *Int J Biochem Cell Biol, 41*(1), 214-224.

Gibbs, D. F., Warner, R. L., Weiss, S. J., Johnson, K. J., & Varani, J. (1999). Characterization of matrix metalloproteinases produced by rat alveolar macrophages. *Am J Respir Cell Mol Biol, 20*(6), 1136-1144.

Glaser, R. (2005). Stress-associated immune dysregulation and its importance for human health: a personal history of psychoneuroimmunology. *Brain Behav Immun, 19*(1), 3-11.

Glaser, R., & Kiecolt-Glaser, J. K. (2005). Stress-induced immune dysfunction: implications for health. *Nat Rev Immunol, 5*(3), 243-251.

Glaser, R., Kiecolt-Glaser, J. K., Marucha, P. T., MacCallum, R. C., Laskowski, B. F., & Malarkey, W. B. (1999). Stress-related changes in proinflammatory cytokine production in wounds. *Arch Gen Psychiatry, 56*(5), 450-456.

Godbout, J. P., & Glaser, R. (2006). Stress-induced immune dysregulation: implications for wound healing, infectious disease and cancer. *J Neuroimmune Pharmacol, 1*(4), 421-427.

Gordon, S. (1995). The macrophage. *Bioessays, 17*(11), 977-986.

Gordon, S. (2003). Alternative activation of macrophages. *Nat Rev Immunol, 3*(1), 23-35.

Gordon, S. (2007). The macrophage: past, present and future. *Eur J Immunol, 37 Suppl 1,* S9-17.

Gordon, S., & Martinez, F. O. (2010). Alternative activation of macrophages: mechanism and functions. *Immunity, 32*(5), 593-604.

Gordon, S., & Taylor, P. R. (2005). Monocyte and macrophage heterogeneity. *Nat Rev Immunol, 5*(12), 953-964.

Gouin, J. P., & Kiecolt-Glaser, J. K. (2011). The impact of psychological stress on wound healing: methods and mechanisms. *Immunol Allergy Clin North Am, 31*(1), 81-93.

Grzanka, A., Misiolek, M., Golusinski, W., & Jarzab, J. (2011). Molecular mechanisms of glucocorticoids action: implications for treatment of rhinosinusitis and nasal polyposis. *Eur Arch Otorhinolaryngol, 268*(2), 247-253.

Guha, M., & Mackman, N. (2001). LPS induction of gene expression in human monocytes. *Cell Signal, 13*(2), 85-94.

Gwinn, M. R., & Vallyathan, V. (2006). Respiratory burst: role in signal transduction in alveolar macrophages. *J Toxicol Environ Health B Crit Rev, 9*(1), 27-39.

Haskill, S., Beg, A. A., Tompkins, S. M., Morris, J. S., Yurochko, A. D., Sampson-Johannes, A., et al. (1991). Characterization of an immediate-early gene induced in adherent monocytes that encodes I kappa B-like activity. *Cell, 65*(7), 1281-1289.

Haskill, S., Johnson, C., Eierman, D., Becker, S., & Warren, K. (1988). Adherence induces selective mRNA expression of monocyte mediators and proto-oncogenes. *J Immunol, 140*(5), 1690-1694.

Hassan, N. F., Campbell, D. E., & Douglas, S. D. (1986). Purification of human monocytes on gelatin-coated surfaces. *J Immunol Methods, 95*(2), 273-276.

He, S., Blomback, M., Bark, N., Johnsson, H., & Wallen, N. H. (2010). The direct thrombin inhibitors (argatroban, bivalirudin and lepirudin) and the indirect Xa-inhibitor (danaparoid) increase fibrin network porosity and thus facilitate fibrinolysis. *Thromb Haemost, 103*(5), 1076-1084.

Hellhammer, D. H., Wust, S., & Kudielka, B. M. (2009). Salivary cortisol as a biomarker in stress research. *Psychoneuroendocrinology, 34*(2), 163-171.

Herbert, J., Goodyer, I. M., Grossman, A. B., Hastings, M. H., de Kloet, E. R., Lightman, S. L., et al. (2006). Do corticosteroids damage the brain? *J Neuroendocrinol, 18*(6), 393-411.

Hesse, M., Modolell, M., La Flamme, A. C., Schito, M., Fuentes, J. M., Cheever, A. W., et al. (2001). Differential regulation of nitric oxide synthase-2 and arginase-1 by type 1/type 2 cytokines in vivo: granulomatous pathology is shaped by the pattern of L-arginine metabolism. *J Immunol, 167*(11), 6533-6544.

Hiscott, J., Marois, J., Garoufalis, J., D'Addario, M., Roulston, A., Kwan, I., et al. (1993). Characterization of a functional NF-kappa B site in the human interleukin 1 beta promoter: evidence for a positive autoregulatory loop. *Mol Cell Biol, 13*(10), 6231-6240.

Horrocks, P. M., Jones, A. F., Ratcliffe, W. A., Holder, G., White, A., Holder, R., et al. (1990). Patterns of ACTH and cortisol pulsatility over twenty-four hours in normal males and females. *Clin Endocrinol (Oxf), 32*(1), 127-134.

Hsing, C. H., Lin, M. C., Choi, P. C., Huang, W. C., Kai, J. I., Tsai, C. C., et al. (2011). Anesthetic propofol reduces endotoxic inflammation by inhibiting reactive oxygen species-regulated Akt/IKKbeta/NF-kappaB signaling. *PLoS One, 6*(3), e17598.

Huang, S., Hendriks, W., Althage, A., Hemmi, S., Bluethmann, H., Kamijo, R., et al. (1993). Immune response in mice that lack the interferon-gamma receptor. *Science, 259*(5102), 1742-1745.

Huang, Y., Krein, P. M., Muruve, D. A., & Winston, B. W. (2002). Complement factor B gene regulation: synergistic effects of TNF-alpha and IFN-gamma in macrophages. *J Immunol, 169*(5), 2627-2635.

Hume, D. A. (2006). The mononuclear phagocyte system. *Curr Opin Immunol, 18*(1), 49-53.

Hume, D. A., Ross, I. L., Himes, S. R., Sasmono, R. T., Wells, C. A., & Ravasi, T. (2002). The mononuclear phagocyte system revisited. *J Leukoc Biol, 72*(4), 621-627.

Hunter, M., Wang, Y., Eubank, T., Baran, C., Nana-Sinkam, P., & Marsh, C. (2009). Survival of monocytes and macrophages and their role in health and disease. *Front Biosci, 14*, 4079-4102.

Huynh, M. L., Fadok, V. A., & Henson, P. M. (2002). Phosphatidylserine-dependent ingestion of apoptotic cells promotes TGF-beta1 secretion and the resolution of inflammation. *J Clin Invest, 109*(1), 41-50.

Iles, K. E., & Forman, H. J. (2002). Macrophage signaling and respiratory burst. *Immunol Res, 26*(1-3), 95-105.

Imhof, B. A., & Aurrand-Lions, M. (2004). Adhesion mechanisms regulating the migration of monocytes. *Nat Rev Immunol, 4*(6), 432-444.

Irwin, M. R. (2008). Human psychoneuroimmunology: 20 years of discovery. *Brain Behav Immun, 22*(2), 129-139.

Ishida, Y., Gao, J. L., & Murphy, P. M. (2008). Chemokine receptor CX3CR1 mediates skin wound healing by promoting macrophage and fibroblast accumulation and function. *J Immunol, 180*(1), 569-579.

Kao, J. S., Fluhr, J. W., Man, M. Q., Fowler, A. J., Hachem, J. P., Crumrine, D., et al. (2003). Short-term glucocorticoid treatment compromises both permeability barrier homeostasis and stratum corneum integrity: inhibition of epidermal lipid synthesis accounts for functional abnormalities. *J Invest Dermatol, 120*(3), 456-464.

Kaplanski, G., Fabrigoule, M., Boulay, V., Dinarello, C. A., Bongrand, P., Kaplanski, S., et al. (1997). Thrombin induces endothelial type II activation in vitro: IL-1 and TNF-alpha-independent IL-8 secretion and E-selectin expression. *J Immunol, 158*(11), 5435-5441.

Kaul, N., & Forman, H. J. (1996). Activation of NF kappa B by the respiratory burst of macrophages. *Free Radic Biol Med, 21*(3), 401-405.

Khallou-Laschet, J., Varthaman, A., Fornasa, G., Compain, C., Gaston, A. T., Clement, M., et al. (2010). Macrophage plasticity in experimental atherosclerosis. *PLoS One, 5*(1), e8852.

Kiecolt-Glaser, J. K., Loving, T. J., Stowell, J. R., Malarkey, W. B., Lemeshow, S., Dickinson, S. L., et al. (2005). Hostile marital interactions, proinflammatory cytokine production, and wound healing. *Arch Gen Psychiatry, 62*(12), 1377-1384.

Kiecolt-Glaser, J. K., Marucha, P. T., Malarkey, W. B., Mercado, A. M., & Glaser, R. (1995). Slowing of wound healing by psychological stress. *Lancet, 346*(8984), 1194-1196.

Kirschbaum, C., & Hellhammer, D. H. (1994). Salivary cortisol in psychoneuroendocrine research: recent developments and applications. *Psychoneuroendocrinology, 19*(4), 313-333.

Kirschbaum, C., Pirke, K. M., & Hellhammer, D. H. (1993). The 'Trier Social Stress Test'--a tool for investigating psychobiological stress responses in a laboratory setting. *Neuropsychobiology, 28*(1-2), 76-81.

Koller, C. A., King, G. W., Hurtubise, P. E., Sagone, A. L., & LoBuglio, A. F. (1973). Characterization of glass adherent human mononuclear cells. *J Immunol, 111*(5), 1610-1612.

Kudielka, B. M., Hellhammer, D. H., & Wust, S. (2009). Why do we respond so differently? Reviewing determinants of human salivary cortisol responses to challenge. *Psychoneuroendocrinology, 34*(1), 2-18.

Kueber, U., Wirtz, P.H., Sakai, M. Stemmer, A., & Ehlert, U. (submitted). A simple in vitro method to investigate microbcidal potential of human macrophages.

Kun, J. F. (2003). Regulation of nitrogen monoxide production in human malaria. *Redox Rep, 8*(5), 289-291.

Kwon, N. S., Nathan, C. F., Gilker, C., Griffith, O. W., Matthews, D. E., & Stuehr, D. J. (1990). L-citrulline production from L-arginine by macrophage nitric oxide synthase. The ureido oxygen derives from dioxygen. *J Biol Chem, 265*(23), 13442-13445.

Landsman, L., Varol, C., & Jung, S. (2007). Distinct differentiation potential of blood monocyte subsets in the lung. *J Immunol, 178*(4), 2000-2007.

Lazarus, R. S. (1986). *Stress, appraisal, and coping.* New York: Springer.

Lazarus, R. S. & Folkman, S. (1984). *Stress, appraisal, and coping.* New York: Springer Publishing Company.

Leibovich, S. J., & Ross, R. (1975). The role of the macrophage in wound repair. A study with hydrocortisone and antimacrophage serum. *Am J Pathol, 78*(1), 71-100.

Li, X., & Stark, G. R. (2002). NFkappaB-dependent signaling pathways. *Exp Hematol, 30*(4), 285-296.

Lopansri, B. K., Anstey, N. M., Weinberg, J. B., Stoddard, G. J., Hobbs, M. R., Levesque, M. C., et al. (2003). Low plasma arginine concentrations in children with cerebral malaria and decreased nitric oxide production. *Lancet, 361*(9358), 676-678.

Lucas, T., Waisman, A., Ranjan, R., Roes, J., Krieg, T., Muller, W., et al. (2010). Differential roles of macrophages in diverse phases of skin repair. *J Immunol, 184*(7), 3964-3977.

Lundberg, U. (2000). Catecholamines. In G. Fink (Ed.). *Encyclopedia of Stress* (pp. 408-413). San Diego: CA: Academic Press.

MacDonald, K. P., Palmer, J. S., Cronau, S., Seppanen, E., Olver, S., Raffelt, N. C., et al. (2010). An antibody against the colony-stimulating factor 1 receptor depletes the resident subset of monocytes and tissue- and tumor-associated macrophages but does not inhibit inflammation. *Blood, 116*(19), 3955-3963.

MacMicking, J. D., Nathan, C., Hom, G., Chartrain, N., Fletcher, D. S., Trumbauer, M., et al. (1995). Altered responses to bacterial infection and endotoxic shock in mice lacking inducible nitric oxide synthase. *Cell, 81*(4), 641-650.

Mahdavian Delavary, B., van der Veer, W. M., van Egmond, M., Niessen, F. B., & Beelen, R. H. (2011). Macrophages in skin injury and repair. *Immunobiology, 216*(7), 753-762.

Mamessier, E., Milhe, F., Guillot, C., Birnbaum, J., Dupuy, P., Lorec, A. M., et al. (2007). T-cell activation in occupational asthma and rhinitis. *Allergy, 62*(2), 162-169.

Mantovani, A., Sica, A., Sozzani, S., Allavena, P., Vecchi, A., & Locati, M. (2004). The chemokine system in diverse forms of macrophage activation and polarization. *Trends Immunol, 25*(12), 677-686.

Marin, V., Montero-Julian, F. A., Gres, S., Boulay, V., Bongrand, P., Farnarier, C., et al. (2001). The IL-6-soluble IL-6Ralpha autocrine loop of endothelial activation as an intermediate between acute and chronic inflammation: an experimental model involving thrombin. *J Immunol, 167*(6), 3435-3442.

Martin, P. (1997). Wound healing--aiming for perfect skin regeneration. *Science, 276*(5309), 75-81.

Martinez, F. O., Gordon, S., Locati, M., & Mantovani, A. (2006). Transcriptional profiling of the human monocyte-to-macrophage differentiation and polarization: new molecules and patterns of gene expression. *J Immunol, 177*(10), 7303-7311.

Martinez, F. O., Sica, A., Mantovani, A., & Locati, M. (2008). Macrophage activation and polarization. *Front Biosci, 13*, 453-461.

McEwen, B. S. (1998). Protective and damaging effects of stress mediators. *N Engl J Med, 338*(3), 171-179.

Midwood, K. S., Williams, L. V., & Schwarzbauer, J. E. (2004). Tissue repair and the dynamics of the extracellular matrix. *Int J Biochem Cell Biol, 36*(6), 1031-1037.

Mildner, A., Schmidt, H., Nitsche, M., Merkler, D., Hanisch, U. K., Mack, M., et al. (2007). Microglia in the adult brain arise from Ly-6ChiCCR2+ monocytes only under defined host conditions. *Nat Neurosci, 10*(12), 1544-1553.

Miller, D. B., & O'Callaghan, J. P. (2002). Neuroendocrine aspects of the response to stress. *Metabolism, 51*(6 Suppl 1), 5-10.

Mirza, R., DiPietro, L. A., & Koh, T. J. (2009). Selective and specific macrophage ablation is detrimental to wound healing in mice. *Am J Pathol, 175*(6), 2454-2462.

Moore, R. Y., & Eichler, V. B. (1972). Loss of a circadian adrenal corticosterone rhythm following suprachiasmatic lesions in the rat. *Brain Res, 42*(1), 201-206.

Morel, F., Doussiere, J., & Vignais, P. V. (1991). The superoxide-generating oxidase of phagocytic cells. Physiological, molecular and pathological aspects. *Eur J Biochem, 201*(3), 523-546.

Mori, R., Kondo, T., Nishie, T., Ohshima, T., & Asano, M. (2004). Impairment of skin wound healing in beta-1,4-galactosyltransferase-deficient mice with reduced leukocyte recruitment. *Am J Pathol, 164*(4), 1303-1314.

Mosser, D. M. (2003). The many faces of macrophage activation. *J Leukoc Biol, 73*(2), 209-212.

Mosser, D. M., & Zhang, X. (2008). Activation of murine macrophages. *Curr Protoc Immunol, Chapter 14*, Unit 14 12.

Murray, H. W., & Cohn, Z. A. (1980). Macrophage oxygen-dependent antimicrobial activity. III. Enhanced oxidative metabolism as an expression of macrophage activation. *J Exp Med, 152*(6), 1596-1609.

Murray, P. J., & Wynn, T. A. (2011). Obstacles and opportunities for understanding macrophage polarization. *J Leukoc Biol, 89*(4), 557-563.

Muthu, K., Deng, J., Gamelli, R., Shankar, R., & Jones, S. B. (2005). Adrenergic modulation of cytokine release in bone marrow progenitor-derived macrophage following polymicrobial sepsis. *J Neuroimmunol, 158*(1-2), 50-57.

Nagalski, A., & Kiersztan, A. (2010). [Physiology and molecular mechanism of glucocorticoid action]. *Postepy Hig Med Dosw (Online), 64*, 133-145.

Nagamura-Inoue, T., Tamura, T., & Ozato, K. (2001). Transcription factors that regulate growth and differentiation of myeloid cells. *Int Rev Immunol, 20*(1), 83-105.

Nagaoka, T., Kaburagi, Y., Hamaguchi, Y., Hasegawa, M., Takehara, K., Steeber, D. A., et al. (2000). Delayed wound healing in the absence of intercellular adhesion molecule-1 or L-selectin expression. *Am J Pathol, 157*(1), 237-247.

Narkiewicz, K., Winnicki, M., Schroeder, K., Phillips, B. G., Kato, M., Cwalina, E., et al. (2002). Relationship between muscle sympathetic nerve activity and diurnal blood pressure profile. *Hypertension, 39*(1), 168-172.

Nathan, C., & Shiloh, M. U. (2000). Reactive oxygen and nitrogen intermediates in the relationship between mammalian hosts and microbial pathogens. *Proc Natl Acad Sci U S A, 97*(16), 8841-8848.

Navarro, S., Debili, N., Bernaudin, J. F., Vainchenker, W., & Doly, J. (1989). Regulation of the expression of IL-6 in human monocytes. *J Immunol, 142*(12), 4339-4345.

Ortega, E., Garcia, J. J., Saez, M. C., & De la Fuente, M. (2000). Changes with aging in the modulation of macrophages by norepinephrine. *Mech Ageing Dev, 118*(3), 103-114.

Owens, M. J., & Nemeroff, C. B. (1991). Physiology and pharmacology of corticotropin-releasing factor. *Pharmacol Rev, 43*(4), 425-473.

Pacak, K., & Palkovits, M. (2001). Stressor specificity of central neuroendocrine responses: implications for stress-related disorders. *Endocr Rev, 22*(4), 502-548.

Padgett, D. A., Marucha, P. T., & Sheridan, J. F. (1998). Restraint stress slows cutaneous wound healing in mice. *Brain Behav Immun, 12*(1), 64-73.

Palermo-Neto, J., de Oliveira Massoco, C., & Robespierre de Souza, W. (2003). Effects of physical and psychological stressors on behavior, macrophage activity, and Ehrlich tumor growth. *Brain Behav Immun, 17*(1), 43-54.

Papadelis, C., Kourtidou-Papadeli, C., Vlachogiannis, E., Skepastianos, P., Bamidis, P., Maglaveras, N., & Pappasa, K. (2003). Effects of mental workload and caffeine on catecholamines and blood pressure compared to performance variations. *Brain and Cognition, 51*, 143-154.

Paulnock, D. M. (1994). The molecular biology of macrophage activation. *Immunol Ser, 60*, 47-62.

Pelegrin, P., & Surprenant, A. (2009). Dynamics of macrophage polarization reveal new mechanism to inhibit IL-1beta release through pyrophosphates. *EMBO J, 28*(14), 2114-2127.

Perretti, M., & D'Acquisto, F. (2009). Annexin A1 and glucocorticoids as effectors of the resolution of inflammation. *Nat Rev Immunol, 9*(1), 62-70.

Persoons, J. H., Moes, N. M., Broug-Holub, E., Schornagel, K., Tilders, F. J., & Kraal, G. (1997). Acute and long-term effects of stressors on pulmonary immune functions. *Am J Respir Cell Mol Biol, 17*(2), 203-208.

Peskin, A. V., & Winterbourn, C. C. (2000). A microtiter plate assay for superoxide dismutase using a water-soluble tetrazolium salt (WST-1). *Clin Chim Acta, 293*(1-2), 157-166.

Pfeifer, M. A., Weinberg, C. R., Cook, D., Best, J. D., Reenan, A., & Halter, J. B. (1983). Differential changes of autonomic nervous system function with age in man. *Am J Med, 75*(2), 249-258.

Pinel, J. P. J. (2009). *Biopsychology* (7th ed.). Boston: Pearson.

Popova, A., Kzhyshkowska, J., Nurgazieva, D., Goerdt, S., & Gratchev, A. (2011). Pro- and anti-inflammatory control of M-CSF-mediated macrophage differentiation. *Immunobiology, 216*(1-2), 164-172.

Porcheray, F., Viaud, S., Rimaniol, A. C., Leone, C., Samah, B., Dereuddre-Bosquet, N., et al. (2005). Macrophage activation switching: an asset for the resolution of inflammation. *Clin Exp Immunol, 142*(3), 481-489.

Pullar, C. E., Grahn, J. C., Liu, W., & Isseroff, R. R. (2006). Beta2-adrenergic receptor activation delays wound healing. *FASEB J, 20*(1), 76-86.

Pullar, C. E., Rizzo, A., & Isseroff, R. R. (2006). beta-Adrenergic receptor antagonists accelerate skin wound healing: evidence for a catecholamine synthesis network in the epidermis. *J Biol Chem, 281*(30), 21225-21235.

Rabinovitch, M., & DeStefano, M. J. (1973). Macrophage spreading in vitro. I. Inducers of spreading. *Exp Cell Res, 77*(1), 323-334.

Rahman, A., Anwar, K. N., True, A. L., & Malik, A. B. (1999). Thrombin-induced p65 homodimer binding to downstream NF-kappa B site of the promoter mediates endothelial ICAM-1 expression and neutrophil adhesion. *J Immunol, 162*(9), 5466-5476.

Restituto, P., Galofre, J. C., Gil, M. J., Mugueta, C., Santos, S., Monreal, J. I., et al. (2008). Advantage of salivary cortisol measurements in the diagnosis of glucocorticoid related disorders. *Clin Biochem, 41*(9), 688-692.

Reyes-Garcia, M. G., & Garcia-Tamayo, F. (2009). A neurotransmitter system that regulates macrophage pro-inflammatory functions. *J Neuroimmunol, 216*(1-2), 20-31.

Robles, T. F. (2007). Stress, social support, and delayed skin barrier recovery. *Psychosom Med, 69*(8), 807-815.

Robles, T. F., Brooks, K. P., & Pressman, S. D. (2009). Trait positive affect buffers the effects of acute stress on skin barrier recovery. *Health Psychol, 28*(3), 373-378.

Rodero, M. P., & Khosrotehrani, K. (2010). Skin wound healing modulation by macrophages. *Int J Clin Exp Pathol, 3*(7), 643-653.

Rogan, M. P., Geraghty, P., Greene, C. M., O'Neill, S. J., Taggart, C. C., & McElvaney, N. G. (2006). Antimicrobial proteins and polypeptides in pulmonary innate defence. *Respir Res, 7*, 29.

Rojanasakul, Y., Ye, J., Chen, F., Wang, L., Cheng, N., Castranova, V., et al. (1999). Dependence of NF-kappaB activation and free radical generation on silica-induced TNF-alpha production in macrophages. *Mol Cell Biochem, 200*(1-2), 119-125.

Rojas, I. G., Padgett, D. A., Sheridan, J. F., & Marucha, P. T. (2002). Stress-induced susceptibility to bacterial infection during cutaneous wound healing. *Brain Behav Immun, 16*(1), 74-84.

Ross, R. (1999). Atherosclerosis--an inflammatory disease. *N Engl J Med, 340*(2), 115-126.

Rouppe van der Voort, C., Kavelaars, A., van de Pol, M., & Heijnen, C. J. (1999). Neuroendocrine mediators up-regulate alpha1b- and alpha1d-adrenergic receptor subtypes in human monocytes. *J Neuroimmunol, 95*(1-2), 165-173.

Rouppe van der Voort, C., Kavelaars, A., van de Pol, M., & Heijnen, C. J. (2000). Noradrenaline induces phosphorylation of ERK-2 in human peripheral blood mononuclear cells after induction of alpha(1)-adrenergic receptors. *J Neuroimmunol, 108*(1-2), 82-91.

Roy, S., Khanna, S., Yeh, P. E., Rink, C., Malarkey, W. B., Kiecolt-Glaser, J., et al. (2005). Wound site neutrophil transcriptome in response to psychological stress in young men. *Gene Expr, 12*(4-6), 273-287.

Rozanski, A., Blumenthal, J. A., Davidson, K. W., Saab, P. G., & Kubzansky, L. (2005). The epidemiology, pathophysiology, and management of psychosocial risk factors in cardiac practice: the emerging field of behavioral cardiology. *J Am Coll Cardiol, 45*(5), 637-651.

Saarialho-Kere, U. K. (1998). Patterns of matrix metalloproteinase and TIMP expression in chronic ulcers. *Arch Dermatol Res, 290 Suppl*, S47-54.

Sakai, M., Vonderheit, A., Wei, X., Kuttel, C., & Stemmer, A. (2009). A novel biofuel cell harvesting energy from activated human macrophages. *Biosens Bioelectron, 25*(1), 68-75.

Sawyer, R. T., Strausbauch, P. H., & Volkman, A. (1982). Resident macrophage proliferation in mice depleted of blood monocytes by strontium-89. *Lab Invest, 46*(2), 165-170.

Schartl, M., Gessler, M., & Eckardstein, A. (2009). *Biochemie und Molekularbiologie des Menschen*. Elsevier: München.

Scheinman, R. I., Cogswell, P. C., Lofquist, A. K., & Baldwin, A. S., Jr. (1995). Role of transcriptional activation of I kappa B alpha in mediation of immunosuppression by glucocorticoids. *Science, 270*(5234), 283-286.

Schneemann, M., & Schoeden, G. (2007). Macrophage biology and immunology: man is not a mouse. *J Leukoc Biol, 81*(3), 579; discussion 580.

Schneemann, M., & Schoedon, G. (2002). Species differences in macrophage NO production are important. *Nat Immunol, 3*(2), 102.

Schroder, K., Hertzog, P. J., Ravasi, T., & Hume, D. A. (2004). Interferon-gamma: an overview of signals, mechanisms and functions. *J Leukoc Biol, 75*(2), 163-189.

Segal, B. H., Han, W., Bushey, J. J., Joo, M., Bhatti, Z., Feminella, J., et al. (2010). NADPH oxidase limits innate immune responses in the lungs in mice. *PLoS One, 5*(3), e9631.

Serbina, N. V., Jia, T., Hohl, T. M., & Pamer, E. G. (2008). Monocyte-mediated defense against microbial pathogens. *Annu Rev Immunol, 26*, 421-452.

Sharma, S., Sharma, M., & Bose, M. (2009). Mycobacterium tuberculosis infection of human monocyte-derived macrophages leads to apoptosis of T cells. *Immunol Cell Biol, 87*(3), 226-234.

Siddiqi, M., Garcia, Z. C., Stein, D. S., Denny, T. N., & Spolarics, Z. (2001). Relationship between oxidative burst activity and CD11b expression in neutrophils and monocytes from healthy individuals: effects of race and gender. *Cytometry, 46*(4), 243-246.

Singer, A. J., & Clark, R. A. (1999). Cutaneous wound healing. *N Engl J Med, 341*(10), 738-746.

Sivamani, R. K., Pullar, C. E., Manabat-Hidalgo, C. G., Rocke, D. M., Carlsen, R. C., Greenhalgh, D. G., et al. (2009). Stress-mediated increases in systemic and local epinephrine impair skin wound healing: potential new indication for beta blockers. *PLoS Med, 6*(1), e12.

Slauch, J. M. (2011). How does the oxidative burst of macrophages kill bacteria? Still an open question. *Mol Microbiol, 80*(3), 580-583.

Sluiter, J. K., van der Beek, A. J., & Frings-Dresen, M. H. (1998). Work stress and recovery measured by urinary catecholamines and cortisol excretion in long distance coach drivers. *Occup Environ Med, 55*(6), 407-413.

Smedes, F., Kraak, J. C., & Poppe, H. (1982). Simple and fast solvent extraction system for selective and quantitative isolation of adrenaline, noradrenaline and dopamine from plasma and urine. *J Chromatogr, 231*(1), 25-39.

Sporn, S. A., Eierman, D. F., Johnson, C. E., Morris, J., Martin, G., Ladner, M., et al. (1990). Monocyte adherence results in selective induction of novel genes sharing homology with mediators of inflammation and tissue repair. *J Immunol, 144*(11), 4434-4441.

Stanojevic, S., Mitic, K., Vujic, V., Kovacevic-Jovanovic, V., & Dimitrijevic, M. (2007). Exposure to acute physical and psychological stress alters the response of rat macrophages to corticosterone, neuropeptide Y and beta-endorphin. *Stress, 10*(1), 65-73.

Steer, J. H., Kroeger, K. M., Abraham, L. J., & Joyce, D. A. (2000). Glucocorticoids suppress tumor necrosis factor-alpha expression by human monocytic THP-1 cells by suppressing transactivation through adjacent NF-kappa B and c-Jun-activating transcription factor-2 binding sites in the promoter. *J Biol Chem, 275*(24), 18432-18440.

Stein, M., Keshav, S., Harris, N., & Gordon, S. (1992). Interleukin 4 potently enhances murine macrophage mannose receptor activity: a marker of alternative immunologic macrophage activation. *J Exp Med, 176*(1), 287-292.

Stout, R. D. (2010). Editorial: macrophage functional phenotypes: no alternatives in dermal wound healing? *J Leukoc Biol, 87*(1), 19-21.

Stout, R. D., Jiang, C., Matta, B., Tietzel, I., Watkins, S. K., & Suttles, J. (2005). Macrophages sequentially change their functional phenotype in response to changes in microenvironmental influences. *J Immunol, 175*(1), 342-349.

Stout, R. D., & Suttles, J. (2004). Functional plasticity of macrophages: reversible adaptation to changing microenvironments. *J Leukoc Biol, 76*(3), 509-513.

Straub, R. H., Westermann, J., Scholmerich, J., & Falk, W. (1998). Dialogue between the CNS and the immune system in lymphoid organs. *Immunol Today, 19*(9), 409-413.

Stroncek, J. D., & Reichert, W. M. (2008). Overview of Wound Healing in Different Tissue Types.

Stuehr, D. J., & Marletta, M. A. (1985). Mammalian nitrate biosynthesis: mouse macrophages produce nitrite and nitrate in response to Escherichia coli lipopolysaccharide. *Proc Natl Acad Sci U S A, 82*(22), 7738-7742.

Subramaniam, M., Saffaripour, S., Van De Water, L., Frenette, P. S., Mayadas, T. N., Hynes, R. O., et al. (1997). Role of endothelial selectins in wound repair. *Am J Pathol, 150*(5), 1701-1709.

Sweet, M. J., Stacey, K. J., Kakuda, D. K., Markovich, D., & Hume, D. A. (1998). IFN-gamma primes macrophage responses to bacterial DNA. *J Interferon Cytokine Res, 18*(4), 263-271.

Tacke, F., & Randolph, G. J. (2006). Migratory fate and differentiation of blood monocyte subsets. *Immunobiology, 211*(6-8), 609-618.

Takahashi, H. K., Iwagaki, H., Mori, S., Yoshino, T., Tanaka, N., & Nishibori, M. (2004). Beta 2-adrenergic receptor agonist induces IL-18 production without IL-12 production. *J Neuroimmunol, 151*(1-2), 137-147.

Takashiba, S., Van Dyke, T. E., Amar, S., Murayama, Y., Soskolne, A. W., & Shapira, L. (1999). Differentiation of monocytes to macrophages primes cells for lipopolysaccharide stimulation via accumulation of cytoplasmic nuclear factor kappaB. *Infect Immun, 67*(11), 5573-5578.

Tan, A. S., & Berridge, M. V. (2000). Superoxide produced by activated neutrophils efficiently reduces the tetrazolium salt, WST-1 to produce a soluble formazan: a simple colorimetric assay for measuring respiratory burst activation and for screening anti-inflammatory agents. *J Immunol Methods, 238*(1-2), 59-68.

Tarling, J. D., Lin, H. S., & Hsu, S. (1987). Self-renewal of pulmonary alveolar macrophages: evidence from radiation chimera studies. *J Leukoc Biol, 42*(5), 443-446.

Taylor, B. S., & Geller, D. A. (2000). Molecular regulation of the human inducible nitric oxide synthase (iNOS) gene. *Shock, 13*(6), 413-424.

Taylor, P. R., Martinez-Pomares, L., Stacey, M., Lin, H. H., Brown, G. D., & Gordon, S. (2005). Macrophage receptors and immune recognition. *Annu Rev Immunol, 23*, 901-944.

Thiele, A., Kronstein, R., Wetzel, A., Gerth, A., Nieber, K., & Hauschildt, S. (2004). Regulation of adenosine receptor subtypes during cultivation of human monocytes: role of receptors in preventing lipopolysaccharide-triggered respiratory burst. *Infect Immun, 72*(3), 1349-1357.

Tietz, N. (2006). *Tietz textbook of clinical chemistry and molecular diagnostics* (4th ed.). St. Louis: Elsevier Saunders.

Trepel, M. (2004). Neuroanatomie. Struktur und Funktion (3rd ed.). München: Urban & Fischer.

Tsigos, C., & Chrousos, G. P. (2002). Hypothalamic-pituitary-adrenal axis, neuroendocrine factors and stress. *J Psychosom Res, 53*(4), 865-871.

Ulrich-Lai, Y. M., & Herman, J. P. (2009). Neural regulation of endocrine and autonomic stress responses. *Nat Rev Neurosci, 10*(6), 397-409.

Urbach, V., Verriere, V., Grumbach, Y., Bousquet, J., & Harvey, B. J. (2006). Rapid anti-secretory effects of glucocorticoids in human airway epithelium. *Steroids, 71*(4), 323-328.

van der Poll, T., Jansen, J., Endert, E., Sauerwein, H. P., & van Deventer, S. J. (1994). Noradrenaline inhibits lipopolysaccharide-induced tumor necrosis factor and interleukin 6 production in human whole blood. *Infect Immun, 62*(5), 2046-2050.

van Furth, R., Cohn, Z. A., Hirsch, J. G., Humphrey, J. H., Spector, W. G., & Langevoort, H. L. (1972). The mononuclear phagocyte system: a new classification of macrophages, monocytes, and their precursor cells. *Bull World Health Organ, 46*(6), 845-852.

van Furth, R., Nibbering, P. H., van Dissel, J. T., & Diesselhoff-den Dulk, M. M. (1985). The characterization, origin, and kinetics of skin macrophages during inflammation. *J Invest Dermatol, 85*(5), 398-402.

van Furth, R., & Sluiter, W. (1986). Distribution of blood monocytes between a marginating and a circulating pool. *J Exp Med, 163*(2), 474-479.

Verhoeckx, K. C., Doornbos, R. P., van der Greef, J., Witkamp, R. F., & Rodenburg, R. J. (2005). Inhibitory effects of the beta-adrenergic receptor agonist zilpaterol on the LPS-induced production of TNF-alpha in vitro and in vivo. *J Vet Pharmacol Ther, 28*(6), 531-537.

Walburn, J., Vedhara, K., Hankins, M., Rixon, L., & Weinman, J. (2009). Psychological stress and wound healing in humans: a systematic review and meta-analysis. *J Psychosom Res, 67*(3), 253-271.

Welch, M. P., Odland, G. F., & Clark, R. A. (1990). Temporal relationships of F-actin bundle formation, collagen and fibronectin matrix assembly, and fibronectin receptor expression to wound contraction. *J Cell Biol, 110*(1), 133-145.

Werner, S., & Grose, R. (2003). Regulation of wound healing by growth factors and cytokines. *Physiol Rev, 83*(3), 835-870.

Wirtz, P. H., Ehlert, U., Emini, L., & Suter, T. (2008). Higher body mass index (BMI) is associated with reduced glucocorticoid inhibition of inflammatory cytokine production following acute psychosocial stress in men. *Psychoneuroendocrinology, 33*(8), 1102-1110.

Wirtz, P. H., von Kanel, R., Frey, K., Ehlert, U., & Fischer, J. E. (2004). Glucocorticoid sensitivity of circulating monocytes in essential hypertension. *Am J Hypertens, 17*(6), 489-494.

Wlaschek, M., & Scharffetter-Kochanek, K. (2005). Oxidative stress in chronic venous leg ulcers. *Wound Repair Regen, 13*(5), 452-461.

Woods, J. A. (2000). Exercise and neuroendocrine modulation of macrophage function. *Int J Sports Med, 21 Suppl 1*, S24-30.

Yang, E. V., & Glaser, R. (2002). Stress-induced immunomodulation and the implications for health. *Int Immunopharmacol, 2*(2-3), 315-324.

Zhang, Y., Kang, X., Chen, L., Pan, C., Yao, Y., & Gu, Z. Z. (2008). Fiber-packed SPE tips based on electrospun fibers. *Anal Bioanal Chem, 391*(6), 2189-2197.

Zhang, X, & Mosser, D. M. (2008). Macrophage acitvation by endogenous danger signals. *J Pathol, 214 (2)*, 161-178.